Brass Instruments

A
Teacher's Guide
to the
Literature of
Brass Instruments

By MARY RASMUSSEN

APPLEYARD PUBLICATIONS
Box 111
DURHAM, NEW HAMPSHIRE

Also in this series:

A Teacher's Guide to the Literature of Woodwind Instruments

✻

A Teacher's Guide to the Literature of Stringed Instruments
(in preparation)

Printed in the U. S. A. by
The Cabinet Press, Milford, N. H.

TO ROBERT D. KING

PREFACE

Probably the most neglected facet of a music teacher's education is the systematic study of the pedagogical and concert repertory of the instruments he or she will be teaching. This book is designed to facilitate such a study, assuming that if suitable textbooks are available more schools of music will be encouraged to offer a course in the literature of wind instruments, either separately or as part of an instrumental methods class, and to acquire the basic collection of music needed to support it. I also hope that it will find use as a checklist for librarians (high school as well as college) interested in evaluating their collection of brass music and as a guide to assist young teachers and performers in finding their way through the vast amount of published music available to them. Experienced teachers of brass instruments will discover little or nothing new here, but perhaps it will help them organize their material more effectively.

In addition to designating the works in the bibliography as suitable for grade school (g.s.), junior high (j.h.), high school (h.s.) and college (c.), all upper ranges beyond g'' (trumpet and horn), f' (trombone and baritone) and f (tuba) have been noted. For foreign readers it is perhaps useful to know that most youngsters in the United States who play brass instruments begin in grade school when they are about ten or eleven years old; that junior high students are usually between the ages of twelve and fifteen, high school students between the ages of fifteen and eighteen.

In the first edition I included works for brass ensemble with rental parts. These have been dropped from the second edition.

I would like to thank Christopher Leuba for calling to my attention the horn studies of Ernst Paul, F. Chester Roberts for valuable comments on the section on tuba solos, Alan Grishman's class in instrumental literature at the University of New Hampshire for a pair of apt suggestions, and Keith Polk, whose review of the first edition for *Brass Quarterly* was so critical that the editor subliminally lost it, but which at least resulted in several changes in the second edition.

Abbreviations are used for the following imprints:

ABroude	Alexander Broude (New York)
AMP	Associated Music Publishers (New York)
Avant	Avant Music (Los Angeles — agent: WIM)
Barnhouse	C. L. Barnhouse (Oskaloosa, Iowa — agent: Sesac)
Belwin	Belwin (Rockville Centre, N. Y.)
Boosey	Boosey & Hawkes (London; Oceanside, N. Y.)
Breitkopf	Breitkopf & Härtel (Wiesbaden, Leipzig — U. S. agent: AMP)
Brogneaux	Editions Musicales Brogneaux (Brussels — U.S. agent: Elkan)
BroudeB	Broude Bros. (New York)
BVK	Bärenreiter-Verlag (Kassel)
CeBeDeM	Centre Belge de Documentation Musicale (Brussels — U.S. agent: Elkan)
CFischer	Carl Fischer (New York)
Chappell	Chappell (London, New York)
Clarke & Way	Clarke & Way (New York)
CML	Chamber Music Library (New York — agent: Fox)
Colin	Charles Colin (New York)
Cor	Cor Publishing Co. (Massapequa, N. Y.)
Cundy-B	Cundy-Bettoney (Boston — agent: CFischer)
Doblinger	Musikverlag Doblinger (Vienna — U.S. agent: AMP)
Donemus	Stichting Donemus (Amsterdam — U.S. agent: Peters)
Durand	Durand (Paris — U.S. agent: Elkan-V)
Elkan	Henri Elkan (Philadelphia)
Elkan-V	Elkan-Vogel Co. (Philadelphia)
EMT	Editions Musicales Transatlantiques (U.S. agent: Presser)
EMusicus	Edition Musicus (New York)
Ensemble	Ensemble Publications (Buffalo, N. Y.)
Eschig	Editions Max Eschig (Paris — U.S. agent: AMP)
FColombo	Franco Colombo (New York)
Fox	Sam Fox Pub. Co. (New York)
Galaxy	Galaxy Music Corp. (New York)
General	General Music Pub. Co. (New York — agent: Boston Music Co.)

GMI	Gosudarstvennoe Muzykal'noe Izdatel'stvo (Moscow —U.S. agent: Leeds)
GSchirmer	G. Schirmer (New York)
Hansen	Wilhelm Hansen (Copenhagen — U.S. agent: GSchirmer)
Heinrichshofen	Heinrichshofen's Verlag (Wilhelmshaven — U.S. agent: Peters)
Henn-C	Edition Henn-Chapuis (Geneva)
Hinrichsen	Hinrichsen Edn. (London — U.S. agent: Peters)
(HM)	(Hortus Musicus)
Hof	Friedrich Hofmeister (Hofhaim/Taunus, Frankfurt/ Main, Leipzig)
Holly-Pix	Holly-Pix Music Pub. Co. (N. Hollywood, Calif. — agent: WIM)
IMC	International Music Co. (New York)
Interlochen	Interlochen Press (Interlochen, Mich. — agent: Crescendo Music Sales Co., Chicago)
Kendor	Kendor Music (Delevan, N. Y.)
Leduc	Alphonse Leduc (Paris)
Leeds	Leeds Music Corp. (New York)
Lemoine	Henry Lemoine (Paris — U.S. agent: Elkan-V)
Lienau	Robert Lienau (Berlin-Lichterfelde — U.S. agent: Peters)
Louisville	Louisville House (Louisville, Ky.)
Marks	E. B. Marks (New York)
Maurer	Editions Maurer (Brussels)
MBQ	Montreal Brass Quintet
McG&M	McGinnis & Marx (New York)
Mentor	Mentor Music (New York — agent: Fox)
Mercury	Mercury Music Corp. (New York — agent: Presser)
Merseburger	Verlag Merseburger (Berlin)
Mills	Mills Music (New York)
Moeck	Hermann Moeck Verlag (Celle)
MRara	Musica Rara (London)
Nagel	Nagels Verlag (Nagels Musik-Archiv) (Kassel — U.S. agent: AMP)
Noetzel	O. H. Noetzel Verlag (Wilhelmshaven — U.S. agent: Peters)
Oxford	Oxford University Press (London; Fair Lawn, N. J.)

Paterson	Paterson's Publications (London — U.S. agent: CFischer)
Peer	Peer International Corp. (New York)
Pelikan	Musikverlag zum Pelikan (Zurich)
Peters	C. F. Peters (New York, Leipzig)
Piedmont	Piedmont Music Co. (New York — agent: Marks)
Presser	Theodore Presser (Bryn Mawr, Pa.)
PWM	Polskie Wydawnictwo Muzyczne (Cracow — U.S. agent: Sesac)
Remick	Remick Music Corp. (New York)
RKing	Robert King Music Co. (North Easton, Mass.)
Rochester	Rochester Music Pubrs. (Fairport, N. Y.)
Rongwen	Rongwen Music (New York — agent: BroudeB)
Rubank	Rubank (Chicago)
Rufer	Rufer Verlag (Gütersloh)
Salabert	Editions Salabert (Paris — U.S. agent: FColombo)
SchottL	Schott & Co. (London — U.S. agent: AMP)
SchottM	B. Schotts Söhne (Mainz — U.S. agent: AMP)
Shawnee	Shawnee Press (Delaware Water Gap, Pa.)
Sikorski	Hans Sikorski (Hamburg — U.S. agent: FColombo)
Simrock	N. Simrock (Hamburg — U.S. agent: AMP)
SouthernNY	Southern Music Pub. Co. (New York)
SouthernSA	Southern Music Co. (San Antonio, Texas)
Summy-B	Summy-Birchard Pub. Co. (Evanston, Ill.)
Templeton	Templeton Pub. Co. (agent: Shawnee)
Tenuto	Tenuto Publications (Hattiesburg, Miss. — agent: Presser)
Tritone	Tritone Press (Hattiesburg, Miss. — agent: Presser)
Universal	Universal Edition (Vienna — U.S. agent: Presser)
UniversalL	Universal Edition (London — U.S. agent: Presser)
Williams	Joseph Williams (London — agent: Galliard, U.S. agent: Galaxy)
WIM	Western International Music (Los Angeles)
Witmark	M. Witmark and Sons (New York)
WMüller	Süddeutscher Musikverlag (Willy Müller) (Heidelberg — U.S. agent: Peters)
Zimmermann	Wilhelm Zimmermann (Frankfurt/Main — U.S. agent: Peters)

TABLE OF CONTENTS

    (Methods and Studies, 67-71; Trumpet Ensembles, 71-74; Horn Ensembles, 74-77; Trombone Ensembles, 77-79; Mixed Duos, 80; Mixed Trios, 80-82; Mixed Quartets, 82-85; Mixed Quintets, 85-88; Larger Mixed Ensembles, 88-90; Brass Choir, 90-92; Trumpet Solos, 92-97; Horn Solos, 97-100; Trombone Solos, 100-103; Tuba Solos, 104)

Chapter I

Methods and Studies

It is not the purpose of this chapter to outline a detailed course of study for any particular pupil, but rather to enumerate and describe a very limited group of representative methods and books of etudes which together over a period of a number of years will assist the student in developing a systematic, comprehensive technique on his particular instrument. Most of the instrumental music teachers for whom this book is intended will probably do little private teaching themselves, especially of advanced students; but they should at least be generally familiar with what is currently being published, or, perhaps of equal importance, what is not being published. In using etudes there are two basic problems: that teachers keep on teaching from familiar ones long after they have become obsolete, and that even the most recent studies always seem several musical generations behind the times and rarely provide the material one needs to make one's teaching relevant to what is actually going on in the world of music. It is a situation not likely to improve, but teachers should at least be alert to the fact that it exists.

Trumpet Methods and Studies

As a beginning method for the group instruction of grade school or junior high pupils, this writer perfers either John Kinyon's *Breeze-Easy* series or Walter Beeler's *Play Away!* As far as making a choice is concerned, there is almost nothing that makes one better than the other. Both are attractive, systematic, very easy — and very conventional — with many familiar tunes. *Breeze-Easy* has a second volume for a second-semester or second-year class which may be used just as well after the *Play Away!* volume.

1

With a private student one might begin with either of the above, changing over to Beeler's *Method for the Cornet* as soon as the easier book begins to progress too slowly. For both private and group pupils Robert W. Getchell's *First Book of Practical Studies* provides good short supplementary material, if it is needed, with a useful balance between legato and tongued studies in a variety of styles, articulations and keys. It's a pretty stodgy diet, though, and one can only lament that there is almost nothing available for young students that shows any awareness of the great changes which have taken place in the last one-hundred years, both in music and in pedagogy.

*

For junior high school students who have had a year or more of instruction, the last three volumes of the Sigmund Hering trumpet course *(The Advancing Trumpeter, The Progressing Trumpeter, The Achieving Trumpeter)* provide a lot of pleasant and purposeful material (but with their little ostrich heads cozily in the sand as far as the twentieth century is concerned). (Incidentally, the first volume of this series, *The Beginning Trumpeter,* would be this writer's choice for a college-level trumpet class for prospective teachers. It is more sophisticated and less juvenile than other beginning methods.) Colin and Bower's *Rhythms* — played "square" or jazz-style — are uncommonly useful little two-line exercises. If a teacher instills early the notion that a good player can control both rhythmic styles at will, he spares himself a lot of anguish later on — and here is the ideal place to do it. Of the conventional intermediate etudes Getchell's *Second Book of Practical Studies* is a simple continuation of the first volume, perhaps most useful as beginning practice in C transposition. P. Clodomir's *70 Little Studies* are very short and easy to teach from, good for a variety of basic aspects of trumpet technique, notably precise tonguing and accuracy of short slurs. The Schantl-Pottag collection of *Preparatory Melodies* is low and more idiomatic for horn than for trumpet, but it has a very good coverage of keys and traditional rhythmic figures, the studies are of a manageable length (about a half page each), and they demand close attention to numerous tempo, dynamic and articulation markings, which are nearly as profuse as similar directions in contemporary scores. For a fairly advanced student Mary van der Woude's *Pre Virtuoso Studies* are useful for practice in rather intricate rhythms and contemporary solfège. Although they are gauchely written, and only the best ones are worth studying, they are almost indispensable simply because there seems to be nothing else available at an intermediate level of difficulty that offers comparably relevant exposure to any basic twentieth-century problems.

*

A talented high school student will find a number of challenging contemporary studies in Everett Gates' *Odd Meter Etudes* (the title explains the contents) and van der Woude's *Advanced Virtuoso Works* (for solfège and multiple subdivisions of the beat). If he masters these, Ernst August Friese's *Neuzeitliche Studien* are a logical next step, but they present really very difficult problems of accuracy, range and rhythm, and they are quite beyond most high school students. (The studies in the second volume are somewhat less demanding, but also less interesting, than those in the first.) For sight reading Dufresne's *Develop Sight Reading* is apt (the studies are too dull to practice, all one *can* do is sight-read them) and Himie Voxman's *Selected Studies* provides a lot of conventional etudes in a single inexpensive volume. For specific problems, the Bordogni-Porret *24 Vocalises* are useful for legato playing; Walter Smith's *Lip Flexibility* for lip slurs, arpeggios and trills; Canty's *Bugle Signals, Calls and Marches* for double tonguing; August Schaefer's *The Professional's Key* for triple tonguing; Robert Nagel's *Speed Studies* for finger dexterity; and Bousquet's *36 Celebrated Studies* for fluent, tuneful, conventional etudes of a moderate length and tessitura — for a student who needs a little ego-building before plunging into the more difficult etudes, and as transposition studies for C and D trumpet. A well-established student might also consider the Arban-Maire *Célèbre méthode complète* a worthwhile long-term investment.

*

At the college level Theo Charlier's *36 Etudes transcendantes* are difficult French etudes, rather conventional in their idiom and in their approach to the trumpet; and Marcel Bitsch's *20 Etudes,* Pierre Max Dubois' *12 Etudes variées,* Charles Chaynes' *15 Etudes* and Roger Boutry's *12 Etudes de virtuosité* are more abstract studies in contemporary French style. Walter Smith's *Top Tones* offer valuable exercise in the very high register. Sigfrid Karg-Elert's *Etüden-Schule,* Op. 41 for oboe can be studied by a trumpeter with a good command of his instrument up to high *d′′′*, and brings to the repertory some very musical etudes for general style and interpretation. And the hot-shot trumpeter who is certain he can play anything and everything might well be put to work on something like Karg-Elert's 25 *Capricen und Sonate*, Op. 153 or Eugène Bozza's *12 Etudes-caprices* (both for saxophone).

Horn Methods and Studies

For a class of beginning hornists Kinyon's *Breeze-Easy* series and Walter Beeler's *Play Away!* are as efficient with horns as they are with trumpets. A private student might begin with either of these, changing over to Marvin Howe's *Method for the French Horn* as soon as the easier volume begins to progress too slowly. For both private and group pupils Bernhard Krol's *Studies for French Horn, Elementary Grade (Waldhorn-Studien für die Unterstufe)*, Getchell's *First Book of Practical Studies* and the first volume of Ernst Paul's *Waldhornschule* are valuable supplementary material. The Krol is unusually fine for its emphasis on embouchure-building slurs and contemporary solfège and rhythmic problems, the Getchell provides a good variety of conventional fare in a reasonably wide range of keys, and the Paul demands considerable agility in its valveless exercises as well as interpretative, expressive playing right from the very beginning.

*

For a junior high student who has had a year or more of instruction and who has real talent, a strong embouchure, lots of money and a good professional teacher, the first volume of Lucien Thévet's *Méthode complète* is probably the best there is; but it is big, bulky, and costs about ten dollars. For a promising and agile *cor basse* the *50 neue melodische Etüden* which are the second volume of Paul's method are fine for solfège, rhythm, phrasing, and varied keys; but they progress very quickly and are best with a teacher who likes to spend quite a bit of time on each individual etude. Less well-endowed students can seek solace and an expanded technique in Getchell's *Second Book of Practical Studies* or in Thévet's *60 Etudes*. The Getchell studies often need supplementing with some high- and low-register exercises because their range is so limited. The Thévet are not as attractively melodious, but they give the student with a strong embouchure better practice in the range *e''* to *g''*.

*

For a high school student, with or without both volumes of the Thévet method, the Schantl-Pottag *Preparatory Melodies,* Thévet's *65 Etudes-déchiffrages,* the first four volumes of Maxime-Alphonse's *200 Etudes nouvelles,* Paul's *50 neue melodische Etüden* (again), and Mary van der Woude's *Pre Virtuoso Studies* provide a well-balanced diet. The Schantl are traditional, nineteenth-century studies, very idiomatic, with excellent coverage of keys and basic rhythmic patterns, demanding close attention to numerous tempo, dynamic and articulation markings. The Thévet are intended as sight-reading studies, but they are also very useful as short etudes for contemporary solfège and rhythm. The Maxime Alphonse are probably *the* most often-used etudes, and sooner or later they touch on almost every aspect of valve-horn technique of the nineteenth and early twentieth century. The Paul were discussed in the previous sub-section. At this stage the later ones are really superb for low horn. The van der Woude are musically awkward and uneven in their interest, but the best are very useful for contemporary problems of solfège and multiple subdivisions of the beat. One should also work on transposition, which should be begun early, even before high school, as soon as the student is secure in his fingerings and pitches from, say, *g* to *e''*.* Thévet, in his method, even advocates that horn players begin by reading their exercises in mezzo-soprano clef, so as always to hear them at the actual pitch. This also accustoms the student early to a C clef, making it more natural for him to transpose by clef — in many ways a faster and more reliable procedure than transposing by interval. Youngsters can adapt very quickly to playing in various clefs, provided that their use is begun early enough. Only when the student has become so used to a particular clef that reading in a new one presents a serious setback to his reading fluency does one encounter much resistance. One can begin very simply, having the student transpose his way through the tunes in the *Breeze-Easy* books and then through the Getchell studies,

---

*Be sure to show the youngster a good picture of an old natural horn with its set of crooks (there is an excellent one in Morley Pegge's *The French Horn,* plate III) when he begins transposing. It is worth hours of explaining.

which are especially good for this because their narrow, central tessitura allows the student to take them up or down quite a distance before they are out of range.

Exceptionally skillful students might even acquire enough technique for the more difficult contemporary studies in van der Woude's *Advanced Virtuoso Works* or Alain Weber's *13 Etudes;* and they will find good supplementary scale, arpeggio and interval studies in the first volume of Paul's *100 technische Studien.*

*

For college or conservatory students Verne Reynolds' *48 Etudes,* Charles Chaynes' *15 Etudes* and Marcel Bitsch's *12 Etudes* are challenging contemporary studies; Eugène Bozza's *18 Etudes en forme d' improvisation* are fine for a light, agile technique; Reynolds' *16 Studies after Kreutzer* demand extreme agility over a very wide range; Heinz Liebert's *25 Spezialstudien* are good for low horn; the second volume of Paul's *100 technische Studien* makes available scale and arpeggio studies over an enormous compass (but the open-horn exercises are not as good as the ones in Thévet's method); and Jean Devémy's *21 Lectures-études,* Charles Conord's *45 Etudes,* and Paul's *60 neue Etüden* are useful transposition studies (untransposed, the latter are also useful as advanced etudes of a moderate tessitura).

Trombone (and Baritone) Methods and Studies

Again, for a class of beginning trombonists, Kinyon's *Breeze-Easy* series and Walter Beeler's *Play Away!* are as good as any. For a private student one might begin with either of these, transferring to Beeler's *Method for the Trombone* as soon as the easier volume begins to move too slowly. For both private and group pupils Jaroslav Cimera's *221 Progressive Studies* are useful, short supplementary exercises in a variety of keys.

*

For junior high students who are not beginners, the second volume of Beeler's *Method for the Trombone* plus Colin and Bower's *Rhythms* and the conventional studies of either H. A. VanderCook's *Etudes* or Sigmund Hering's *40 Progressive Etudes* make up a rather uninspiring curriculum, but there seems to be nothing better. There simply are no good intermediate studies published for trombone — at least none with any relevance to the needs of today's teachers. In theory this writer likes the capsule technique builders in Colin's *Progressive Technique,* while wishing they weren't so completely conventional in rhythm and tonality. Pupils, alas, seem to loathe them. With a fairly advanced student van der Woude's *Pre Virtuoso Studies* are useful for aspects of contemporary solfège and rhythm, and Himie Voxman's *Selected Studies* provide lots of conventional etudes for sight-reading.

*

With skilled high school or inexperienced college students the old one-two punch of the Bordogni-Rochut *Melodious Etudes* for legato technique, tone and phrasing, and Blèger's *31 Brilliant Studies* for staccato tonguing is still hard to beat. To these one should add Blazhevich's *Clef Studies* and perhaps Dufresne's *Develop Sight Reading.* Some specific problems can be dealt with via several of the special studies for trumpet, notably Smith's *Lip Flexibility;* Canty's *Bugle Signals, Calls and Marches* for double tonguing; and Schaefer's *The Professional's Key* for triple tonguing. Advanced students should investigate Blazhevich's *Sequences,* which afford more study in contemporary solfège and rhythm, and perhaps André Lafosse's *Méthode complète,* although the latter is not nearly as good as its counterparts for trumpet (Arban-Maire) and horn (Thévet).

A student with a bass trombone or a tenor trombone with an F attachment will find either Allen Ostrander's *The F Attachment and Bass Trombone* or his *Method for Bass Trombone and F Attachment* very helpful, and either of these can profitably be followed by Reginald Fink's edition of Blume's *36 Studies.*

*

For college or conservatory students Marcel Bitsch's *15 Etudes de rhythme* and Kauko Kahila's *Advanced Studies* are worthwhile contemporary etudes. Roger Boutry's *12 Etudes de haut perfectionnement* and Gérard Pichaureau's *20 Etudes* are welcome but not outstanding, the latter demanding more or less the ultimate in conventional technique, without a great deal of sophistication to go with it. Bass trombonists should investigate the "10 [i.e. 12] Etudes modernes" by contemporary French composers at the back of Paul Bernard's *Méthode* and Ostrander's *Shifting Meter Studies*. It is a pity that the studies in the Bernard cannot be purchased separately. Seven dollars is a lot to pay for a dozen etudes, however useful they may be.

*

Baritone horn players should learn both bass and treble clefs and study from both trombone and trumpet material. Note that Beeler has a separate *Method for Baritone* and Voxman a separate volume of *Selected Studies*.

Tuba Methods and Studies

Tuba players start out, at least, like everyone else, and teachers can use Kinyon's *Breeze Easy* series, Beeler's *Play Away!* and *Method for the Tuba,* and Getchell's two books of *Practical Studies* in the same way one would use them for a young trumpeter. These should keep the student supplied through junior high, and after that there is really little to choose from. High school students are perhaps best served by Jaroslav Cimera's *73 Advanced Tuba Studies* and Allen Ostrander's *Shifting Meter Studies,* while college and conservatory players will find Blazhevich's *70 Studies,* Vasil'ev's *Etudes,* and Otto Maenz's *12 Spezialstudien* technically (but not musically) challenging. Shed no tear for the poor tuba student. He learns early on to borrow trumpet and trombone etudes and usually masters the various clefs far better than players who really need to know them.

Chapter II

Music for Ensembles of Like Instruments

A discussion of duets for two like instruments logically follows one of methods and studies because many duets can be looked upon simply as "etudes for two"; and some facets of the student's technique, notably rhythmic ensemble and Baroque style, can be developed better from duets than from solo etudes. In this writer's experience there is no substitute, when teaching, for having a complete personal library of music on hand at all times. And when beginning to teach at any particular level it is good preparation actually to lay out all of the suitable material so that one can see just what is available in various styles and for various technical problems. By setting out duets as well as etudes one often finds that, even for brass instruments, there really is a rich and interesting variety of music of both pedagogical and artistic interest to use at almost every stage of instruction.

However, when using duets as supplementary etudes one should remember that it is generally not sound pedagogy to play duets with the student during his lesson. Most teachers who do are merely getting in some extra practice of their own at the student's expense. On the other hand, there are times when duets are useful in teaching balance, intonation and style; and they are excellent sight-reading practice because the student is forced to keep going at a tempo not necessarily of his own choosing. Also, emotionally disturbed or very timid youngsters sometimes respond better to a lesson of duets than to one of playing alone.

Trumpet Duets

For grade school or junior high school pupils who have become moderately fluent on their instruments many of the little recorder collections yield attractive, easy duets (and the small 16mo booklets fit comfortably and safely in an instrument case).* René Matthes' anthology of little pieces *From a Music Book of 1740 (Aus einem Spielbuch von 1740)*† is a good introductory selection. Willy Schneider's *Erstes Trompetenspiel* is similar, but in larger format (oblong octavo), and includes solos, duets and trios — some with optional percussion. This very easy collection has the advantage of being usable right along with an elementary method, but the pieces are not as attractive as the ones in many of the other collections — mainly, of course, because they must be kept so simple. Four small booklets of folk-songs which are especially nice for young trumpeters are Erich Doflein's *Der Fuchstanz und andere Volkstänze*†, Adolf Hoffmann's *Deutsche Dorfmusik*†, Emanuel Voreck's *Volkstänze aus dem Bayrischen Wald*† and Viktor Korda's *Volksmusik aus Oesterreich*†. Four similar publications, but of Baroque and Classical pieces, are Doflein's two volumes of *Leichte Duette*†, Willy Schneider's *Klassische Spielstücke*† and Arthur von Arx's arrangement of *Christmas Music (Kleine Weihnachtsmusik)*† by Esprit-Philippe Chédeville. Of the larger (quarto) collections, Sigmund Hering's *Miniature Classics, More Miniature Classics* and *Trumpets for 2* contain pleasant arrangements, mostly of eighteenth-century keyboard music, which are somewhat more sophisticated and difficult than the pieces in the smaller books and which are perhaps better reserved for junior high. Some of the more demanding ones are even useful with high school students for practice in style, unusual keys and smooth technique. Himie Voxman's two volumes of *Selected Duets* present a batch of nineteenth-century teaching duets (in style, if not in date) plus some arrangements of eighteenth-century pieces. They aren't very interesting, but one gets a lot of notes for not much money, and they are good for conventional sight-reading practice. The first volume is suitable for junior high, the second for high school.

Among the many fine collections of Renaissance bicinia are several which are suitable for novice players, but probably only a teacher with genuine enthusiasm for the music of this period will be able to transmit any of it to his pupils. The pieces in Leopold Nowak's edition of *Bicinien der Renaissance* are among the easiest. The tessitura is low

---

*Throughout this book 16mo collections will be marked with a †. It is sometimes a bit of a surprise to order what one thinks is a substantial collection, only to receive something which almost disappears into one's shirt pocket.

and the rhythms uncomplicated, but the players must adjust their thinking to music written in larger note values, including breves, that is unbarred except for short guidelines between the staves. This is a small effort, really, and many times rewarded by the amount of fine music which can be investigated once it is made. The pieces in Walther Pudelko's edition of *Leichte Duette alter Meister des 16. Jahrhunderts* are easy, but the tessitura is rather high for young players (often with fairly long passages in the range c'' to g''), in a closely spaced texture. About half of the lovely, fluent *Bicinia* by Orlando di Lasso in Gerhard Pinthus' edition are for two treble instruments. They are not as high as the ones in Pudelko's set, and the texture is more varied, but the rhythm tends to be tricky without the bar-lines. The notation of the duets in Helmut Mönkemeyer's *Meister des 16. und 17. Jahrhunderts* has been modernized somewhat (with tiny bar-lines extending only between the second and fourth lines of the staff and with ties written out over them) so it is easier for youngsters to read, and the selections themselves are interesting, but some are rather too long at this stage. Nonetheless, several of the shorter ones might be useful in easing the transition between conventional notation and the more sophisticated practice of the previously mentioned collections. Also useful in this respect are some of the shorter but musically less attractive pieces in Mönkemeyer's edition of selections from Georg Rhaw's *Bicinia gallica et latina*.

One of the unhappier aspects of present-day music publishing is that while many publishers are all too willing to hire an editor to dig up easy music of past centuries (and of almost any quality — good, bad or indifferent) none seems willing to commission anything for young players from composers of the present. A noteworthy exception is Wilhelm Ehmann's *Geistliches Zweierspiel,* a collection of chorale settings by German composers. Most of them are for two treble-clef instruments, although many are for a treble- and a bass-clef instrument. They are good for all ages, from grade school through college, the musical quality is uniformly high, and they offer an introduction to a prominent, if rather conservative, contemporary idiom — one with shifting meters, quartal harmonic and melodic constructions, the open sonorities of fourths and fifths, and some mild dissonance. The sound is very appropriate and they are surprisingly attractive to most young players. From a pedagogical standpoint they present a fine vehicle for the full, declamatory tone required for effective chorale playing. As for other contemporary duets, there seems to be nothing but odds and ends. Erik Norby's two sets of *Three Suites,* the miscellaneous small pieces in his *2-Stemmig Trompetmusik,* and P. Cabus' *Duo* are pleasant, better-than-average school music. Stefania Lachowska's mildly dissonant *Duety* are usable as solfège practice, good for checking if the student really hears what he is playing, but otherwise poorly composed. Among the recorder duets, Hans Poser's *Spiel- und Tanzstücke* are excellent for developing rhythmic independence and accuracy. The tessitura of the upper part is high *(g'* to *g''/a'').* Paul Arma's *Music on French Folk Tunes* has many short movements in a rather conservative contemporary idiom. Both parts are of equal importance and very independent. Henk Badings' *Kleine Suite*[†] is fluent, tasteful and again rather conservative. It is definitely worth doing, but probably only a movement or two at a time because the first part is very high.

*

For high school students the Cassel-Gearhart *Trumpet Sessions* is a lot of fun — a good-natured hodge-podge of rounds, musical curiosities, jazz pieces and some classical and not-so-classical arrangements. It is nice to have lying around the studio or rehearsal room for spontaneous ensemble playing. Its successor, Gearhart's *Duet Sessions,* is more of the same — but less well balanced, with the emphasis on the "cute stuff." A little, one discovers, goes a long way.

As Renaissance borrowings for both high school and college players Jan Pieterszon Sweelinck's *Rimes françoises et italiennes* are flowing and graceful (barred between the staves only); Lasso's *Six Fantasias* are sophisticated pieces with a moderate tessitura in the upper part and a very low one in the lower (barred, with modern ties across the barlines — notation-wise the easiest to read of these three collections); and Dietz Degen's edition of lovely duets from Erasmus Rotenbucher's anthology of *Schöne und liebliche Zwiegesänge* sets them forth without even a hint of a bar-line in a challenging and rewarding test of fine phrasing and breath control. On the lighter side, Carl Dolmetsch's arrangements for two recorders of *Music from Shakespeare's Plays* (short dances and songs in completely modern notation) can be played by two trumpeters, the wide, rapid skips of some of them adding a little technical challenge to pleasant diversion.

High school and college trumpeters are likely to be very interested in the high trumpet parts of Baroque music. Of the hundreds of late-seventeenth-century duets, only Roman Weichlein's are available in a layman's edition. They are a fine introduction to Baroque style and technique for players with sturdy, well-developed high registers; but unless one's student has an unusually strong embouchure it is prudent to work gradually toward such high parts via some of the many collections of recorder duets which are so useful in this context. The little pieces in Fritz Dietrich's selection *Aus Leopold Mozarts Notenbuch*[†], Benoist Guillemant's Suite (1746)[†] and a number of the arrangements in F. J. Giesbert's *Aus dem Barock* are sensible and pleasant preparation for the higher parts, with the range of the first part extending only to *a''*, but centering quite consistently in the tessitura *c''* to *a''*. When the player has become accustomed to this range, try Giesbert's two little volumes of *Barocke Spielstücke*. The upper voice here is just a trifle higher, usually ascending to *bb''* or *c'''*. High register is, of course, not the only problem trumpeters face in playing Baroque music. Ornamentation and improvisation are two others, and although trumpeters do not need the really sophisticated knowledge of Baroque performance practices required of, say, flutists and violinists, they should be able to do more than just smack a trill on the penultimate note of every phrase. Esprit-Phillipe Chédeville's six *Galante Duos* make excellent introductory ornamentation and improvisation studies. There are no problems of range; the little French + abounds, to be replaced by ornaments of the player's choice; and there are many repetitious passages which so obviously benefit from a little added improvisation that students quickly rise to the challenge. Articulation, in the sense of knowing when to tongue and when to slur, is yet another Baroque problem. A good place to start adding slurs, and a good place to practice one's ornamentation while strengthening one's high register, is Philibert de Lavigne's *Two Easy Suites (Zwei leichte Suiten)*, originally for two recorders or other woodwind.

Among contemporary duets for high school students there is unfortunately very little from which to choose. Everett Gates' *Odd Meter Duets* are somewhat of a disappointment because he has backed away from the starker idiom of his *Odd Meter Etudes* into one which is much more conventional. They are still useful rhythmic practice, but they should have been better. Karl Schäfer's *Spielstücke*[†], Arthur Butterworth's *Three Dialogues* and Patrick McMullen's *Three Movements* are useful study pieces — Schäfer's in a quartal idiom with mild dissonance and occasionally shifting meters, Butterworth's rather mild and chromatic, and McMullen's somewhat atonal and challenging for solfège workouts. Finally, several of Jacques Castérède's *Six pièces brèves en duo* are fun for recital or recreation.

*

College and conservatory players might well spend their time more profitably at something other than hunting down trumpet duets, although there are still a few items worth bearing in mind. Johann Walter's *Kanons in den Kirchentönen* are fine Renaissance examples of the art; Giovanni Giacomo Gastoldi's *Spielstücke* are lively, challenging late-sixteenth-century duets and the first of Johann Vierdanck's *Capricci à 2 cornetti* is a stylish little showpiece for two good players. A small word of warning is perhaps in order about the duets of Girolamo Fantini which turn up from time to time (there is an edition of eight of them by John Glasel published by Chamber Music Library [Mentor]). Whatever his other merits may have been, Fantini simply had no talent for composition. From the Baroque the Weichlein *Trompetenduette* mentioned earlier are useful, as are the *Klarinetten-Duette aus der Frühzeit des Instruments* assembled by Heinz Becker, the first five of which were also intended for trumpets. Players with strong high registers (to d''') can show off a little, and practice their ornamentation at the same time, with Joseph Bodin de Boismortier's Sonata, Op. 6, No. 6 — one of the very few Baroque flute duets with movements short enough to be practical for trumpeters. For contemporary duets, nothing new, alas. Max Seeboth's *Drei Duette* and Wolfgang Rebner's *Inventionen* are good mainstream German stuff, but nothing earth-shaking; and Richard de Guide's Duo is just another French piece — but at that they seem to be the pick of the crop.

Trumpet Trios

At the time of the first edition of this book it seemed as though a nice little contemporary repertory was developing for two and three trumpets. Since then, however, almost nothing new has appeared, and it is no longer easy to muster much enthusiasm for the recent literature of either ensemble. Nevertheless, there are a number of nice older trios, especially for young players.

For grade school and junior high ensembles Vincent Knight's collection of *Ten Trios* (folk songs and arrangements of pieces by Nicolai, Beethoven, Handel, Lully and Mendelssohn) and Hans Melchior Brugk's *Zehn kleine Vortragsstücke* (ten little recital pieces) are very good. Both are nicely scored, with a clear, rosy-cheeked sound just right for young players.

*

For junior high and high school Carl Philipp Emanuel Bach's March for three trumpets and timpani and Richard Franko Goldman's collection of *Five Pre-Classical Pieces* for three trumpets and drums are attractive but slight early works; and Victor Herbert's *Just for Fun* for cornet trio, bass and snare drums is one little piece from the Sousa era which still holds some of its naive charm. From the twentieth century there are several easy items, one of the easiest being Herbert Elwell's *Fanfares Strictly for Trumpets*. These are musically rather inconclusive, but a good beginning for quartal writing and changing meters. Karl Schäfer's *Spielstücke*† are also easy and intended specifically for young players. They vary somewhat in quality, but they are a good introduction to contemporary music of a slightly quartal idiom. Vaclav Nelhybel's *Twelve Concert Pieces* and *Musica festiva* are usable as practice pieces for accurate sight-reading, but their shapeless, austere style is too uninteresting for anything more. William Presser's Suite is a gay, conservatively written spoof for recital or recreation.

*

A good high school or college trio will find three of Helmut Mönkemeyer's collections of seventeenth- and eighteenth-century music for recorders very idiomatic for trumpets as well: *Musik aus dem Frühbarock, Musik aus der Vorklassik,* and *Musik aus dem Hochbarock*. Another recorder trio which is nice for trumpets is Edgar Hunt's arrangement of a Suite in G (originally C) by Johann Mattheson. Finding suitable recorder trios to play on trumpets isn't as easy as it might first appear. The writer must have looked at about fifty to come up with these four. The trick is to find one in which all the parts sound as written, an uncommon notation in recorder trios, where usually either the first two parts sound an octave higher or the third an octave lower.

The two *Capricci à 3 cornetti* in Hans Engel's edition of *Capricci* by Johann Vierdanck are very effective when played by three good trumpeters, and Willson Osborne's *Four Fanfares Based on Eighteenth-Century French Hunting Calls* are agile little pieces in a neo-Classical manner. Suitable twentieth-century trios, in the approximate order of their difficulty, are P. Cabus' *Trois Mouvements;* Robert Muczynski's trumpet Trio, Op. 11, No. 1; Leon Stein's Trio; Anthony Donato's Sonatina; Otto Ketting's *"Kleine Suite"* (1957); Henri Tomasi's Suite; Burrill Phillips' Trio and Ernst Levy's *Fanfares* (1947). Of these the only ones with any real personality are the Donato, in a vigorous, approachable, tertian-quartal, rhythmic style; the Phillips, in an abstract, individualistic, rather dissonant idiom; and the Levy, which is based on chant-like melismatic figures. (One semester ought to be about enough for a trumpet trio to exhaust its repertory.)

Trumpet Quartets, Etc.

Much as publishers of educational music seem to be pushing it, the trumpet quartet has no serious or even very useful repertory of its own. There are a few odd lots — like Johann Dismas Zelenka's Baroque *Reiterfanfaren;* Sigismund Neukomm's *Fanfares;* a good arrangement of Samuel Scheidt's lively Canzona, orginally for four cornetti; and Jakob Seiff's *Bayrische Fanfaren* and Peter Streck's *Fränkische Fanfaren,* both reprints of quaint little nineteenth-century collections — but these are mainly of historical or occasional interest.

For larger ensembles the Concerto for (7) clarini and timpani attributed to Johann Ernst Altenburg captures for a moment some of the splendor of the eighteenth-century trumpeter corps; and Ronald Lo Presti's Suite for five trumpets and Verne Reynold's *Music* for five trumpets make a brave contemporary noise when played by very good high school or college players, although they seem to generate more excitement than music.

Horn Duets

One probably doesn't need to worry much about horn duets before the junior high level, but if one does have a pair of very young students who want some nice duets, the best ones in this writer's experience are to be found in Wilhelm Ehmann's *Geistliches Zweierspiel.* These little contemporary chorale settings have a very solemn, noble sound when played by two hornists of any age, and they are also pedagogically useful for encouraging a full, declamatory style of playing.

A pair of junior high or inexperienced high school hornists can have a lot of fun getting started with the lively little French hunting calls in Dietz Degen's *Fröhliche Jagd†*. This is published for two recorders, but the calls are much more suitable for two horns. Otto Stösser's *Duette alter Meister* contains some short, pleasant, eighteenth- and nineteenth-century pieces, but one has to wade through a lot of awful Türrschmiedt duets to find them. Sydney Twinn's *Twelve Old English Songs* presents well-chosen tunes in conservative but very idiomatic settings. Among the easy horn duets by famous composers, Rimsky-Korsakov's *Two Duets* are modest, rather naive, and appropriate for young students, although the quick skips of the second are not easy; Schubert's five Duos are very short and completely inconsequential (they are reprinted in both the Stösser and the Voxman collections); and Rossini's five Duos are stiff and juvenile. From the larger duet collections, Wendell Hoss's *Sixty Selected Duets* includes a number of easy but routine teaching duets, and the first volume of Himie Voxman's *Selected Duets* has a lot of not-too-difficult arrangements of eighteenth-century pieces and nineteenth-century pedagogical duos.

For two high school or college players William Bates' *"Flourishes"* (originally called *Duettinos*) are short, uncomplicated late-eighteenth-century duets. Some of the little duet collections for soprano and alto recorders can provide very challenging parts for horns, and there probably are a lot of them. Two that are especially suitable are Adolf Hoffmann's adaption of *Kleine Stücke†* by Telemann and an anonymous arrangement of pieces by Haydn in a booklet entitled *Kleines Haydn-Heft†*. The second volume of Voxman's *Selected Duets* makes available many eighteenth- and nineteenth-century duets, and it is a handy volume for sight-reading practice. From the twentieth century Ruth Gipps' *A Taradiddle* is a folksy set of variations for two *cors basses*. Rudolph Mayer's *Twelve Bicinia* are bland and rather unimaginative duets in a sometimes quartal idiom. They are excellent solfège training but that's about all. Viktor Korda's five *Bagatellen* are modest and conservative but rather long — not terribly interesting, but what contemporary horn duets are?

For college or very good high school players Hans Erdmann's edition of twenty-four anonymous eighteenth-century *English Duets†* (Longman and Broderip's twenty-four *Select Duets*) have a few chal-

lenging moments, especially for the second horn, and they are good
preparation for the Mozart duets. Frédéric Duvernoy's *Twenty Duets*
are rather simple-minded, turn-of-the-nineteenth-century pieces, but
several are excellent studies for a variety of *batteries de second cor.*
The various duets by Otto Nicolai are at times lustily naive, at times
little more than boring passagework, but they can be profitable flexibility studies. Wilhelm Kopprasch's eight Duets are typical nineteenth-
century teaching duos, something to play, but not much more. Pierre
Métral's *Piéces en duo* are closely scored and quartalish, with a high,
tight sonority. They are not particularly outstanding, but it is difficult
to find better contemporary duets for this level.

Two skilled college or conservatory players may want to sharpen
their accuracy on the wide skips of Verne Reynolds' arrangement of
six viola da gamba sonatas by Johann Schenk, but, technical challenge
aside, this writer finds them musically routine. Mozart's twelve Duets
are delightful, of course, but it takes two very fine players to toss them
off in the sparkling style they deserve. And Gunther Schuller's varied
Duets are demanding contemporary studies or concert pieces.

Horn Trios

The horn trio doesn't have enough repertory to keep an ensemble
alive, but three college or very good high school players might find
the various trios of Anton Reicha's Op. 82, Frédéric Duvernoy's four
Trios and Henry Cowell's *Hymn and Fuguing Tune No. 12* something to play when the fourth of a horn quartet doesn't show up for
rehearsal.

Horn Quartets, Etc.

When one considers how much horn players like to get together and
play quartets there is surprisingly little music that is really worth
playing. The ensembles this writer has observed have begun bravely
enough, but have soon given up for lack of enough repertory to keep
the group going.

Fortunately one rarely has to contend with a grade school horn
quartet, because the school music collections which one must rely on
for easy pieces are uniformly dismal. To launch a group of four inter-

mediate players, Frank Clark's hunting fantasia called *St. Hubert's Hunting Song,* the folk-song settings of Paul Cadow's *Drei Stücke* and the pieces of both kinds in Kurt Janetzky's *Jägerstücklein* are easy and attractive. Herbert Schultz's arrangements of Palestrina's *Christe, lux vera* and Vittoria's *O sacrum convivium* are technically easy, but they require both sophistication and endurance and are perhaps more useful as tone studies for a high school quartet.

At the high school level Nicolas Tcherepnin's six Quartets are lush, Romantic pieces — rather dreadful, really, but very well scored and so much better than most of the rest of the repertory that players keep coming back to them. Rimsky-Korsakov's *Notturno* is a modest, pleasant little sketch. Rossini's *Le Rendez-vous de chasse* is a long hunting-call fantasia, boring if played straight through but a possible light number if played lustily and with appropriate cuts. Rudolph Mayer's *Four Little Pieces* and Walter Rein's *Divertimento* and *Waldmusik* are better-than-average school music. They aren't very interesting, but they are good study pieces, with movements of manageable length.

With a college or very good high school quartet the late eighteenth-, early nineteenth-century quartets by Friedrich Dionys Weber, W. A. Lütgen and Jacques François Gallay are fun to try. Quartets always read through them but never take them very seriously. The first two are quite high for the first horn (plenty of high c''''s); the tessitura of the Gallay is more moderate. Of the contemporary quartets, Ulysses Kay's Serenade No. 2 is a good one to work up and perform. Arthur Harris' Theme and Variations and Ronald Lo Presti's Second Suite are slick, professional jobs — splashy but without a great deal of substance. Richard Arnell's *Music for Horns,* Op. 82 has nine short, rather conservatively scored movements. Most of them are easy to work up and several are good practice pieces for intonation and rhythmic ensemble. Eugène Bozza's Suite; Mario Castelnuovo-Tedesco's *Chorale with Variations,* Op. 162 and Marius Flothuis's *Quattro invenzioni,* Op. 64 (1963) are additional contemporary works which are worth at least a reading. And Albert Harris's Theme and Variations is something to try if one wants to show off eight horn players.

Somewhere along the way very fine hornists ought to get a chance to perform Hindemith's Sonata (1952), Verne Reynolds' *Short Suite,* Michael Tippett's very challenging Sonata and Gunther Schuller's *Five Pieces for Five Horns (1952).*

Trombone Duets

The repertory of duets specifically written for two trombones is a particularly impoverished one, but by being ingenious and wide-ranging in their borrowing, two players, especially good ones, can keep themselves quite well-stocked with fairly respectable music.

The most musically satisfying duets for young players are the four contemporary German chorale settings for two trombones in Ehmann's *Geistliches Zweierspiel*. For junior high or inexperienced high school players there are a lot of teaching duets and arrangements of eighteenth-century pieces in the first volume of Voxman's *Selected Duets*. This is surely one of the dullest collections he has ever assembled, but when one considers the overwhelming mediocrity of the available music perhaps it is remarkable that it is as good as it is. Obviously if trombonists are to find duets worth playing they must look elsewhere. As a first step students should practice reading treble clef parts down an octave and master as well the old trick of adding two flats and reading treble clef as tenor clef, a procedure which often puts treble-clef duets in keys which are less awkward for the trombone. A number of Renaissance instrumental duets are available published in vocal tenor clef, to be played an octave below the treble-clef notation, and most of these are superbly suited to two trombones. Very easy ones can be found in Leopold Nowak's *Bicinien der Renaissance*. As noted above in the discussion of trumpet duets, the tessitura is low and the rhythms uncomplicated, but the players must cope with music written in larger note values, including breves, that is unbarred except for short guide-lines between the staves. This is a small effort, really, and many times rewarded by the amount of fine music which can be investigated once it is made; and, one should add, the performance of these bicinia by trombones is historically much more justifiable than by trumpets. Walther Pudelko's collection of *Leichte Duette alter Meister des 16. Jahrhunderts* is similar to the Nowak, and a good place to practice newly learned reading skills.

High school or college students will find very appropriate Renaissance duets in the first two volumes of Helmut Mönkemeyer's selection from Georg Rhaw's *Bicinia gallica et latina* (vocal tenor clef). The bassoon repertory also occasionally produces some usable duets. Two sets from the turn of the nineteenth century which will give trombonists a lot of healthy exercise are Etienne Ozi's three little Sonatas and Georg Abraham Schneider's Duets. And while one is poaching, Willem de Fesch's Sonatas, Op. 8 are very nice eighteenth-century cello duets which lie reasonably well for two trombones. Of the many grandiose nineteenth-century trombone duets, Victor Cornette's *Six Concert Duets* still hold up well, and high school students seem to enjoy them. From the twentieth century, Vladimir Blazhevich's *Concert Duets* are standard teaching pieces, musically unexciting but very useful for sight-reading, clefs, keys and rhythm. William Russo's Duets, Op. 35 are good for students interested in writing music as well as playing it, with their little examples of various contrapuntal devices, twelve-tone sets, rhythms and styles. The second volume of Voxman's *Selected Duets* is good for sight-reading, and the Gearhart-Cassel-Hornibrook *Bass Clef Sessions* (duets, trios and quartets) provides a lot of recreational material.

There don't seem to be any good published contemporary duets for college- or conservatory-level trombonists, but there are a number of sixteenth- through nineteenth-century duets which can be appropriated from other instruments: sixteenth-century bicinia like Johann Walter's *Kanons in den Kirchentönen* (vocal treble clef) and Orlando di Lasso's two-part Fantasias (vocal treble clef); eighteenth-century duets for two cellos or bassoons like those by Joseph Bodin de Boismortier and Michel Corrette in Heinz Edelstein's two volumes of *Rokoko-Duette* (angularly unidiomatic, but the better practice for it); and turn-of-the-nineteenth-century pieces for bassoons like François Devienne's *Duos concertants,* Op. 3 and François René Gebauer's *Duos concertants,* Op. 8 (fluent and a real challenge to two good players).

Trombone Trios

The trombone trio really doesn't have enough repertory to be worth considering as an independent ensemble. As with the horn trio the chief reason for keeping up-to-date on its music is to have something on hand when a trombone quartet suddenly finds itself without a fourth.

For three high school or very good junior high players Anton Bruckner's *Aequale* is slow, intense and easy; Art Dedrick's arrangement of Antonio Lotti's *Vere languores nostros* nothing one would go out of one's way to play, but a good tone study; Richard Fote's arrangement of a fugue from Schumann's Op. 68 lively fare for agile per-

formers; Paul Tanner's *Imitation* a casual West Coast affair and Raymond Premru's unpretentious, conventional *Two Pieces* usable as ensemble studies.

College players may want to take a look at Daniel Speer's two
seventeenth-century Sonatas; Gotthilf Heinrich Kummer's naive, turn-
of-the-nineteenth-century bassoon Trios; and Raymond Moulaert's
conservative but sonorously scored Suite (1939).

Trombone Quartets, Etc.

Four trombones playing together surely make one of the world's
most beautiful sounds and although the music available for such an
ensemble is quite mediocre, every trombonist ought to have an opportunity to play in a quartet from time to time, if only to enjoy the
sonority.

Junior high players, or grade school ones, for that matter, will find
Eino Olander's Suite a good piece to get started on. It is a musical
nothing, but easy, and scored with mouth-watering lushness. More
excellent training is available in Robert King's collection of *Twenty-
four Early German Chorales*† and Dedrick's arrangement of a *Miserere*
and *Amplius* by Beethoven.

For a high school or inexperienced college quartet there are a number
of very tastefully done arrangements, notably Richard Myers' really
beautiful scoring of *Two Ancient Carols* by Michael Praetorius. His
adaptations of Thomas Morley's madrigals *Now is the Month of Maying*
and *My Bonnie Lass* are surprisingly idiomatic; and Robert King's set
of *Sixteen Chorales* by J. S. Bach is very useful for all occasions. Of the
contemporary works Vaclav Nelhybel's *Three Organa* are easy but
high for the first trombone. They are severely simple pieces requiring a
stark tone quality which is the very antithesis of the lush, rich sound
usually associated with the trombone quartet in works like André
Ameller's *Chorale*. Nelhybel's *Six Pieces* are excellent ensemble training for precise attention to minute detail, although musically they have
little to say. Flor Peeters' Suite, Op. 82; Robert Sanders' *Scherzo and
Dirge* and James Langley's Suite are all contemporary but somewhat
conservative works which are not terribly difficult. A bass trombone is
essential for the fourth part of the Peeters.

For a college or very sophisticated high school quartet Jay Friedman's
adaptation of a *Ricercare del 12° tono* by Andrea Gabrieli, Keith

Brown's of a Sonata by Giovanni Gabrieli and Glenn Smith's of a
Canzona by Biagio Marini provide some digestible late Renaissance
and early Baroque fare, although the editing of the Giovanni Gabrieli
is rather old-fashioned and the Marini is, frankly, a bit of a bore.
Beethoven's *Three Equali* are slow and somber — not difficult, but
high for the first trombone. Mr. Smith's arrangements of two of
Mendelssohn's choruses for male voices betray their vocal antecedents
a little too quickly, but it is nice to have something for trombones from
this period. From the twentieth century Leslie Bassett's Quartet and
Jacques Charpentier's *Quatuor de forme liturgique* are good for concert performance; and Pierre Max Dubois' Quartet, Patrick McCarty's
Recitative and Fugue and Harold Laudenslager's *Three Preludes and
Fugues* are worthwhile rehearsal pieces.

Of the quartets suitable for an experienced college or conservatory
ensemble Roger Chapman's *Suite of Three Cities* is perhaps the best.
None of the rest is particularly outstanding, but the following deserve at least a reading: Ludwig Otten's Suite (1951), Jeanine Rueff's
Deux pièces brèves, Kazimierz Serocki's Suite (1953), Jean-Michel
Defay's *Quatre pièces,* Arthur Meulemans' Suite (1942), Roger Boutry's
Cinq pièces a quatre, David Gow's Suite, Henri Tomasi's *Être ou ne
pas être* and Alan Lumsden's arrangement of an unaccompanied *Concerto a 4* by Telemann.

For more than four trombones Thomas Stoltzer's Fantasia (much
better played by five trombones than by the four trombones and tuba
the editor designates), Paul Tanner's arrangement for six trombones of
Dido's Lament from Henry Purcell's *Dido and Aeneas* (very high
for first trombone), Burrill Phillips' *Piece* for six trombones and Tiburtio Massaino's Canzona for eight are all worth bearing in mind,
and are most likely to be suitable for a college ensemble.

Tuba Duets

Richard Franko Goldman's Duo is a nice serial, atonal work for two
very good, sophisticated tuba players; and Don Butterfield's *Seven
Duos* is a good-natured but challenging pastiche for study or recreation.

Chapter III

Music for Brass Ensembles

Duets — Trumpet and Trombone

Grade school or junior high players will find several easy duets for trumpet and trombone in Wilhelm Ehmann's *Geistliches Zweierspiel* and in Robert King's arrangement of *Four Short Fugues* by Mikhail Ivanovitch Glinka. One ought also to be able to locate a number of nice, simple duets among the pieces for two recorders. The most usable ones are apt to turn up among the duets for soprano and alto or tenor, where the soprano is written to sound an octave higher. Then, if the trombone plays the second part an octave lower instead, the original spacing between the voices will be preserved. This, of course, involves learning to read treble clef an octave lower (if the trumpet plays in C) or as tenor clef (if the trumpet plays in Bb), but both are useful skills which the trombonist will no doubt master sooner or later, so he might as well learn them early and enjoy the easy music they make available to him. Walter Bergmann's arrangement of some *Leichte Handstücke* by James Hook is an example of some easy and idiomatic pieces which can be played this way.

The more sophisticated recorder duets suitable for high school or college players are most likely to have the second part written in vocal tenor clef to sound an octave lower, instead of having the first part sound an octave higher as is the custom in the easy duets. The reading and transposition problems for the trombonist are the same either way. Among the many Renaissance bicinia published for two recorders or simply for two unspecified instruments, Gerhard Pinthus' edition of *Bicinia* by Orlando di Lasso and the third volume of Helmut Mönkemeyer's selection from Georg Rhaw's anthology of *Bicinia gallica et latina* contain a number of pieces very suitable for performance

25

on trumpet and trombone. As for not-too-difficult duets published specifically for trumpet and trombone, there really is very little beyond Art Dedrick's arrangement of the fourteenth of Bach's two-part Inventions and Robert King's French Suite.

For two really fine college players David Borden's *Fifteen Dialogues* are first-rate, angular contemporary duets, good for study or recital; Meyer Kupferman's abstract *Available Forms* (1966) are extremely valuable for practice in complex rhythmic ensemble; René Defossez's *Quatre petits pièces* (1956) are difficult recital duets in a rather conservative idiom; and Elliott Schwartz's *Essays* (1966) are part chance pieces, more avant garde than most music for brass instruments.

Duets — Trumpet and Horn

Of the few published duets for trumpet and horn, Robert King's arrangement of *Four Short Fugues* by Glinka is tasteful and easy; and Jan van Dijk's Serenade (1955) and Andrew Kazdin's *Twelve Duets* are modest, not-too-difficult contemporary works.

Trios — Two Trumpets and Trombone

A trio of young players of two trumpets and a trombone can easily be stocked with music from the recorder trio's repertory. The best pieces to use are the ones for two sopranos and an alto (or tenor) where the two sopranos sound an octave higher than written. With these, if the trumpeters play in C the trombonist must read the third part down an octave. If they play in Bb the trombonist should read his part as though it were written in tenor clef and mentally add two flats. In searching through recorder trios for ones suitable for brass, look for pieces with a low third part so that it will lie comfortably for the trombonist while imparting a richer sonority to the sound of the ensemble as a whole. Some easy collections containing short, attractive pieces which lie well for all the instruments and are ideally suited to junior high or even good grade school players are Erich Katz's *Music of the Baroque,* LaNoue Davenport's arrangement of *Six American Folk Songs,* Katz's *Suite of Jewish Folk Tunes (Chanukah Melodies),* Joel Newman's arrangement of *Fifteen Canzonets* by Salomone Rossi and Alfred Mann's selection of *Six Lively Airs* of Jacob Regnart. As for short, easy pieces published specifically for three brass instruments,

there are several — sacred and secular, old and new — in Fritz Bachmann's *Lass dir unser Lob gefallen.*

A trio of high school or college players may want to investigate the
longer recorder trios and some of the ones with a higher third part,
like Helmut Mönkemeyer's set of *Instrumentale Liedsätze um 1500;*
Davenport's arrangement of *Five Carnival Songs* by Joan Domenico
del Giovane da Nola; Winifred Jaeger's selection of *Five Canzonettas*
by Luca Marenzio, Giovanni Gastoldi and Valentin Haussmann;
Edgar Hunt's *Old English Pieces;* Katz's arrangement of *Five Sinfonie
a tre voci* by Rossi; Jaeger's adaptation of *Three Canzonettas* by Johann Hermann Schein; Johannes Runge's collection of *Barocke
Musizierstücke* and René Colwell's adaptation of two Terzetti by
James Hook. (There is also an enormous amount of three-part vocal
music from the Renaissance which is directly playable with two
trumpets and a trombone. A survey of this vast repertory is quite
beyond the scope of this book, and it must suffice here to cite only
three examples from the *Das Chorwerk* series: Erich Hertzmann's
edition of *Volkstümliche italienische Lieder* [No. 8]; R. B. Lenaerts'
selection of fifteen *Flämische Lieder der Renaissance* [No. 92] and
Anton Gosswin's *Newe teutsche Lieder* [No. 75].) Two thoroughly
enjoyable arrangements, made specifically for brass instruments, are
Robert King's versions of Mozart's Divertimento No. 1 (K. E. 439b)
and Beethoven's Trio, Op. 87. Of the contemporary trios William
Mayer's *Country Fair* — a lively, brassy, rhythmic piece — is most
likely to appeal to high school students. Three more sophisticated
possibilities are José Ardévol's clashing, contrapuntal *Tercera Sonata
a Tres;* Stanley Glasser's Trio (1958) and Vladimir Sramek's toccata-
like Trio. For a church group, or simply for an ensemble wanting
some mature but easy music, there are many contemporary three-part
chorale settings in Wilhelm Ehmann's *Evangelisches Kantoreibuch.*

Trios — Trumpet, Horn and Trombone

While the trio of two trumpets and trombone has (or can find) a
lot of easy music and is better for grade school and junior high students,
the trio of trumpet, horn and trombone has the more interesting difficult
repertory and is the more suitable for college players or for very good
high school ones.

The repertory is largely contemporary, although Conrad de Jong's selection of *Three Josquin Pieces* and King's adaptation of Beethoven's Trio, Op. 87 are available for contrast. Of the easier modern works Francis Poulenc's Sonata (1922) and Robert Marek's Trio are attractive and rather conservatively written — probably the best of the lot. P. Cabus' *Sonata a tre* is vigorous and assertively dissonant; Edgard Leclercq's *Suite classique* and Charles Scharrès' Divertimento are conventional and conservative; while Morris Knight's Cassation, Robert Sanders' Trio and Marius Flothuis's Sonatina, Op. 26 (1945) are cheerfully wrong-noty (the Sanders is, in fact, rather dourly wrong noty). Arthur Meulemans' two trios stand stylistically somewhere in between the last two groups, the first nearer the latter, the second, the former.

Mature, skilled college or conservatory players will no doubt want to attack Jean Louël's angular, somewhat pointillistic, rhythmically explosive Trio (1951), the more conservative exposition of a similar idiom in Marcel Quinet's *Sonate a trois* (1961), and Niels Viggo Bentzon's gently chromatic Trio, Op. 82 (1952). Two other works in a more straight-forward, vigorous idiom are Mark Hughes' wry Divertimento and Karl Kroeger's *Sonata breve* (1957).

Quartets — Two Trumpets and Two Trombones

As any parent who has been dragged off to a grade school or junior high band concert will tell you, most of the music young instrumentalists play in school is of execrable quality. Perhaps one way to infiltrate some good music into the schools would be through an active chamber music program. The trouble with such a program is that it takes so much of a teacher's time per pupil; but with a little ingenuity in enlisting musical parents, students from nearby colleges or even mature high school students, each to "adopt" an ensemble for one or two sessions a week, one might be able to get something going. For young players of brass instruments the ensemble with the greatest variety of easy, interesting music is the quartet of either two trumpets and two trombones or two trumpets, horn and trombone. Enterprising teachers will have their trumpeters learn to play in both C and B♭, their hornists in C and F, and their trombonists in vocal tenor clef as well as bass and tenor clefs so the group can play not only from music published specifically for brass quartet but also from the whole repertory of four-part vocal music and from the almost endless supply of easy pieces for recorder quartet.

For a novice grade school or junior high quartet with trumpets reading in B♭ the arrangements of a *Gagliarda* by Frescobaldi, Purcell's *Music for Queen Mary II* and *Three Dances* from Tilman Susato's *Het derde musyck boexken* are very suitable and usually well-received. Robert King's selection of *Three Hymns* by Palestrina is also extremely easy, but less sure fire.

A junior high quartet or a high school group just getting under way can choose from a large number of tasteful arrangements and editions, of which the following are especially recommended: Giovanni Gabrieli's *Canzona per sonare No. 3* (requires fluent technique); Pietro Lappi's *Canzoni 11 and 12;* Purcell's *Two Trumpet Tunes and Ayre* and his *Allegro and Air from King Arthur;* Gottfried Reiche's Sonata No. 24 and his *Two Sonatas,* Nos. 21 and 22; Johann Georg Christian Störl's Sonata No. 1; Bach's *March, Chorale and Fugue;* Handel's *Bourrée and Minuet;* André Campra's *Rigaudon;* Alexander Glazunov's *In modo religioso;* and King's set of *Three New England Hymns* and his collection of *Reformation Chorales.* Three modest contemporary works also belong here: Alan Hovhaness's *Sharagan and Fugue,* Charles Knox's *Solo for Trumpet with Brass Trio* and Willy Schneider's *Turmmusik.* A quartet reading in C will find many early works as well as conservatively written modern pieces in Fritz Bachmann's *Lass dir unser Lob gefallen* and Hans Martin Schlemm's *Lass dir unser Lob gefallen II,* and mildly dissonant, contemporary chorale settings in Bachmann's *Posaunenchoralbuch.*

For a high school or all-star junior high quartet Neil Butterworth's *Tudor Suite* (works by Gibbons, Palestrina, Morley and John Mundy), Giovanni Gabrieli's *Canzona per sonare No. 2,* Reiche's Sonatas Nos. 18 and 19, and King's arrangement of *Two Pieces* by François Couperin can serve to introduce the players to some of the more sophisticated and challenging early works. Burrill Phillips' *Prelude,* Edmund Haines' *Toccata,* Jean Berger's *Intrada,* Robert Starer's *Dirge* and Houston Bright's *Legend and Canon* are contemporary works of moderate difficulty. Of these the Phillips is musically the most rewarding, the Haines the most immediately attractive. If one of the trombonists can double on baritone Edrich Siebert's *Bees-a-Buzzin'* is a cute little perpetual-motion piece for a pops concert. For a quartet reading in C Hindemith's *Morgenmusik* is a must; and there are a number of interesting chorale-based pieces in Wilhelm Ehmann's collection of *Bläser-Intraden zum Wochenlied.*

Good high school players, or inexperienced college ones, will want to investigate Andrea Gabrieli's *Ricercar* [i.e. Canzona] *del duodecimo tuono,* Giovanni Gabrieli's *Canzona per sonare No. 4,* Reiche's Sonata No. 15 and King's collection of *Twenty-two Chorales* by J. S. Bach. Arthur Frackenpohl's Quartet, Frederick Piket's *Dance and March* and Robert Sanders' Suite are perhaps the dreary best of a dismal lot of twentieth-century works. Morris Knight's *Six Brass Quartets* provide a lot of sight-reading material, but their unreadable score makes them rather impractical for more intensive study.

A skilled college quartet soon discovers that the pickings have become rather slim as far as specifically published works are concerned, although Giovanni Gabrieli's *Canzona per sonare No. 1, "La Spiritata,"* is a work of wonderful rhythmic variety; and the four-part pieces by Valentin Haussmann, Melchior Franck, Michael Praetorius, Johann Staden, Georg Vintz, Isaac Posch and Paul Peuerl in Ehmann's *Alte Spielmusik für Bläser* are unusually well-chosen examples of seventeenth-century German and Austrian instrumental music. Beyond this players should seek out additional music on their own and should become concerned with such matters of performance practice as diminution and tonguing syllables. From the twentieth century Ulysses Kay's *Brass Quartet,* William Bergsma's Suite and Frank Wohlfahrt's *Fanfaren-Musik* (1958) are performable mainstream moderns. (The Kay, it seems, is a piece one either likes very much or can't stand. The writer is of the later persuasion.)

Quartets — Two Trumpets, Horn and Trombone

For a beginning quartet the Frescobaldi, Purcell, Susato and Palestrina pieces listed in the previous sub-chapter are all published with an alternate part for horn. In addition, Sigmund Hering's *Early Classics for Brass Ensembles* contains six very easy arrangements of dances and chorales, and Arnold Bentley's collection of *Sixteenth-Century Quartets* makes available several sophisticated and beautifully scored short pieces. The latter collection may take a little selling, but it is well worth it. Donald Stratton's adaptation of five pieces from Bartok's *For Children* is an attempt to infuse the repertory with something more modern. The result is not very effective and the lower parts are uninteresting, but it was a good try.

For a junior high quartet or a high school group just getting under way all of the arrangements and contemporary works enumerated in the previous sub-chapter come with alternate (or original) horn parts; and the four Canzonas of Orlando di Lasso arranged by Neil Butterworth and Jurriaan Andriessen's neo-Renaissance *Quattro Madrigali* are also mature but easy.

High school or all-star junior high players can use all of the quartets of the previous sub-chapter except the Siebert. In addition, Butterworth's collection of *Four Motets* (by A. Gabrieli, Giuseppe Corsi, Gregor Aichinger and Vittoria) is very good for elegant, independent playing; and Ronald Lo Presti's *Miniature,* Lyndol Mitchell's *Folk Suite* and Gordon Jacob's *Scherzo* are lively modern works. The Lo Presti, though rather slick, is probably the one most likely to succeed with a high school group.

Good high school players, or inexperienced college ones, can look into Giovanni Gabrieli's *Canzona per sonare No. 4* and Butterworth's arrangement of *Mr. Curch's Toye and Other Pieces* by Thomas Tomkins for seventeenth-century works; Wilhelm Ramsoe's Quartet No. 5 for a quaint, nineteenth-century period piece; and Andriessen's *Introduzione e allegro* and John Addison's Divertimento, Op. 9 for moderately difficult, rather conservative contemporary numbers. Lewis Raymond's *Short Suite* is a good study project for careful attention to dynamics and a variety of articulations, although less promising as a recital offering.

With a skilled college quartet John Boda's *Prelude/Scherzo/Postlude,* John Gardner's Theme and Variations, Op. 7 (1951) and Homer Keller's Quartet are playable but not very exciting, more-or-less mainstream works; Donald H. White's Serenade No. 3 is a good serial piece; and Joep Straesser's *"Music for Brass"* (1965) is the closest the brass quartet gets, among the published works, to something avant garde.

Quintets — Two Trumpets, Horn and Two Trombones

Although the brass quartet has the best music for beginners and is the ideal chamber music ensemble for novices, the brass quintet has the best advanced repertory and is more satisfactory for older students. Nevertheless, there is some good, easy music for a quintet, especially for a quintet of two trumpets, horn and two trombones; and to launch one of, say, junior high pupils Robert King's transcriptions of *Two Pieces* by William Brade, *Two Pieces* by Anthony Holborne and *Three Pieces* by Johann Pezel, and John Corley's arrangement of Purcell's (i.e. Clarke's) *Trumpet Voluntary* are all easy and fun to play.

For high school or older junior high players John Adson's *Two Ayres for Cornetts and Sagbuts,* King's transcription of *Five Pieces* by Holborne and his selection of *Six Pieces* by Pezel, Pezel's Sonatas Nos. 2 and 3, and Corley's arrangement of Purcell's *Voluntary on Old 100th* are approachable early works; and Ludwig Maurer's *Scherzo* and *Lied* are charming nineteenth-century pieces.

The repertory for a college or very good high school quintet is a bit more varied. Pezel's Sonata No. 22 and the anonymous Bänkelsänger Sonata are interesting seventeenth-century pieces; Harry Freedman's arrangement of *Four Madrigals* by Carlo Gesualdo is good for intonation practice, although perhaps too obviously vocal for concert performance; Robert Nagel's selection of *Three Pieces* by Maurer and Victor Eval'd's Quintet are richly scored, serenely nineteenth-century pieces (even though the Eval'd was composed after the end of the century); and Collier Jones' *Four Movements for Five Brass* (1957) and Paul Whear's *Invocation and Study* are not-too-difficult contemporary works. For a concertizing quintet Arnold Fromme's editions of Reiche's Quartets Nos. 11 and 12 are useful. They are for trumpet and three trombones, but there are several substitute parts and quintets will find them handy for giving one of the trumpets a rest. They are rather over-edited to this writer's taste, but very cleverly marked so that they can be performed effectively with a minimum of rehearsal. Two other quartets which are useful in the same way are King's arrangement of Jacob Obrecht's *Tsat een Meskin* and William Presser's *Five Southern Songs.*

For a skilled college quintet the complete editions of Pezel's *Fünff-stimmigte blasende Music* and *Hora decima* provide volumes of interesting music, and Fromme's arrangement of Michael East's *Desperavi* is a very sophisticated single work. Luigi Zaninelli's *Designs* is a modest contemporary piece, valuable for a long program because various sections are scored for just two or three instruments, giving the others more chance to rest than they usually get. Of the more difficult contemporary works Robert Sanders' Quintet in Bb major, Ingolf Dahl's *Music for Brass Instruments* (1944) and Irwin Bazelon's *Brass Quintet* (1963) are all good for study or concert.

Quintets — Two Trumpets, Horn, Trombone and Tuba

A quintet of two trumpets, horn, trombone and tuba is not a practical ensemble for very young players because the tuba is hardly a small boy's instrument, so one usually does not need to worry about music for such a group until junior high or even high school, where works like Don Ross's arrangement of Beethoven's *Prayer, Op.* 48, No. 1; Irving Rosenthal's adaptation of *Three Chorale Preludes* by Brahms; Wilfred Roberts' casual, popular-style fantasy on *Dixie;* his *Three Headlines* and William Schmidt's modest, contemporary *Variations on a Negro Folk Song* are good to start out with. Furthermore, if the tuba player has a good high register or is resourceful about adapting second trombone parts, all of the easy pieces enumerated in the previous sub-chapter can be studied by a quintet with trombone and tuba instead of two trombones.

For a college quintet, or a very good high school one, Walter Hartley's Quintet (1963) is a first-rate work in his own angular, dissonant style; William Schmidt's Suite No. 1 is vigorous and rhythmic, in a distinctly American idiom; and Morley Calvert's *Suite from the Monteregian Hills* is an effective light concert number. Other works worth investigating are Victor Eval'd's lushly Romantic Quintet, Hartley's *Divertissement* (1965), and Samuel Baron's *Impressions of a Parade, Based on "When Johnny Comes Marching Home Again."* There are also two editions of Pezel's Sonatas, Nos. 5 and 27, scored for a quintet with horn and tuba; and Clifton Williams' arrangement of two of Schumann's *Kinderszenen* is useful for variety on a school concert by a touring ensemble.

A good college or conservatory quintet will find Collier Jones' *Four Movements for Five Brass* (1957) and John Huggler's Quintet good mainstream contemporary works for concert or chamber music study; Fisher Tull's *Exhibition* and Barney Childs' *Variations sur une chanson de canotier* very useful demonstration pieces for a group giving school programs; Malcolm Arnold's Quintet an unusually well-written casual number and John Glasel's edition of *Three Pieces* by Holborne some fine, contrasting, older music. Other works worth looking into by a quintet that rehearses regularly are Samuel Adler's *Five Movements;* Eugène Bozza's Suite (1967), Sonatina and *Suite française* (all with high French tuba parts); Arthur Frackenpohl's *Brass Quintet;* Arthur Harris's *Four Moods* (1957); Ton de Kruyf's *Aubade* (1957-1967); Albert Cobine's *Trilogy* (very high for first trumpet) and Earl Zindars' Quintet. A concertizing ensemble might want to keep in its repertory some pieces like the Zaninelli *Designs* noted in the previous subchapter or Leonard Bernstein's *Fanfare for Bima* (trumpet, horn, trombone and tuba), which gives a trumpeter a chance to sit one out.

For a really professional quintet Gunther Schuller's *Music for Brass Quintet* (1961) and Alvin Etler's Quintet (1963) are impressive and very difficult display pieces; and, in the same vein, Schuller's *Little Brass Music* (1963) (trumpet, horn, trombone and tuba) can be used to give one of the trumpets a rest.

Quintets — Two Trumpets and Three Trombones or Three Trumpets and Two Trombones

A quintet made up only of trumpets and trombones is of course a very practical ensemble to have when good horn players are in short supply, but it has more positive virtues as well, being the best ensemble for the performance of much of the late Renaissance and early Baroque music so abundantly available, and having the most suitable instrumentation for a church-affiliated group. It is especially important that the trumpet players in this ensemble be able to read in C as well as in B♭ — and, if three trombones are used, that the first trombone have a strong high register and be able to read treble clef — so that they can make use of the many fine German collections. In fact, the best place to find good music for a beginning ensemble is Hans Martin Schlemm's *Lass dir unser Lob gefallen II,* which contains a large number of easy pieces, both sacred and secular. This collection alone could keep a church group stocked with music for several years. Two separate publications also suitable for a quintet just getting under way are King's edition of *Two Pieces* by Anthony Holborne and John Adson's *Two Ayres for Cornetts and Sagbuts.*

A college or very good high school quintet will find many sacred and secular pieces in Fritz Bachmann's *Lass dir unser Lob gefallen* plus a number of rather conservatively contemporary German chorale settings in Wilhelm Ehmann's *Bläser-Intraden zum Wochenlied.* In addition, several of the separately published arrangements and editions can be played by a quintet of two trumpets and three trombones, provided the first trombone is strong, including the anonymous Bänkelsänger Sonata, Giovanni Gabrieli's *Canzona prima a 5,* Brade's *Two*

Pieces and Holborne's *Five Pieces*. From the twentieth century Werner Hübschmann's *Musik* is a typical but unusually ambitious German work. A really intellectual group will want to learn how to add diminutions to the upper parts, and the well-chosen five-part pieces in Ehmann's *Alte Spielmusik* are good places to begin applying them.

A skilled college quintet should work very hard on its diminutions and improvisation, and might even want to try using cornetts for the upper parts. Such an ensemble will find publications like the complete editions of Pezel's *Hora Decima* and *Fünff-stimmigte blasende Music,* Matthew Locke's *Music for his Majesty's Sackbuts and Cornetts,* Charles Coleman's *Four Pieces for Sackbuts and Cornetts* and John Glasel's selection of *Three Pieces* by Holborne all worthwhile additions to its library, and beyond these there is an almost endless amount of five-part music awaiting transcription in the various *Denkmäler* series.

Sextets

There is almost no instrumentation in between the brass quintet and the big brass choir with enough respectable music to sustain a recital or study group. It will therefore, with only one or two exceptions, best serve the purpose of this book merely to enumerate those single works most likely to be performed or studied for some isolated reason rather than as part of the repertory of a continuing ensemble.

The sonority of the old brass sextet (two trumpets, horn, trombone, baritone and tuba) is too woolly to attract good contemporary works at the moment, but of the older ones John Verrall's Suite has well but conservatively written short movements which can very pleasantly be played by junior high or high school players; and Oskar Böhme's Sextet in E-flat minor, Op. 30 is a lush, nineteenth-century work, ideally suited to its medium, but so long and full of flats that it isn't very practical except as a period piece for college players. Philip Bezanson's *Prelude and Dance* (2121) is often found on college programs, probably because it won the 1960-61 *Nacwapi* competition. This writer finds its dense motivic construction a bore. Paul Cadow's *Intrada* (2220) is an easy example of German school music. Robert King's arrangement of *Three Pieces* from Handel's *Water Music* (3210/2220) is popular with junior high and high school groups wanting to show off a pair (or more) of good horns.

Of the various possible sextet combinations, that of three trumpets and three trombones seems at present to be the only one with any real pedagogical and musical possibilities, especially for a church ensemble or a sort of *collegium musicum* specializing in Renaissance and early Baroque music. (The trumpet players must be able to read in C.) At the junior high or high school level there are a lot of easy six-part sacred and secular pieces in Bachmann's *Lass dir unser Lob gefallen* and Schlemm's *Lass dir unser Lob gefallen II.* Among the separate publications Hans Melchior Brugk's *Fanfare und Intrade* and Karl Pilss's *Vier Fanfaren* are unpretentious examples of conservatively contemporary German school music. High school or college ensembles will find a number of modern chorale settings in Ehmann's *Bläser-Intraden zum Wochenlied* and several fine seventeenth-century pieces in his *Alte Spielmusik für Bläser* and in Thurston Dart's *Suite from the Royal Brass Music of King James I.* Skilled and sophisticated ensembles will want also to investigate Matthew Locke's *Music for King Charles II* and Karl Kroeger's contemporary *Canzona III.*

Septets

One could, if one had to, put together a little program of music for a septet of upper brass in pairs plus tuba (2221), with Giovanni Battista Buonamente's toccata-like Sonata, Pierre Max Dubois' short and flashy *Trois préludes en fanfare,* Rolf Scheurer's conservatively written *Scherzo* (with timpani) and Nicolai Berezowsky's *Brass Suite,* Op. 24. It would be a light and lively affair, without much real contrast, and best at the college level. For other septet combinations, Hans Melchior Brugk's Suite (3031-timp) and Max Seeboth's Suite (4030) are sonorous, conservative contemporary works for junior high or high school players. Orlando di Lasso's *Providebam dominum* (4030) and Carl Ruggles' *Angels* (4030) are important and sophisticated pieces for college students (the rhythmic ensemble in the Ruggles is fiendishly elusive).

Octets

The various eight-part canzoni of Giovanni Gabrieli (4040, etc.) are the perfect accompaniment to a particularly festive occasion. Of the separately published editions, the *Canzon primi toni* and *Canzon septimi toni No. 2* of 1597 are perhaps most likely to be successful with high school (as well as college) players. A college ensemble may also find useful the Canzoni Nos. 27 and 28 of 1608 and the more somber *Sonata pian' e forte*. These antiphonal works should not be undertaken lightly, it being this writer's experience that it takes a lot of rehearsing to achieve a really satisfactory spacing and coordination of the two choirs. On a more mundane level, Jaromir Weinberger's *Concerto for the Timpani* (4040-timp) used to be a popular high school piece which has now come to sound rather passé, although it is perhaps still usable on a light concert.

Nonets

For good college players Chou Wen-Chung's *Soliloquy of a Bhiksuni* (1431-perc) can add some exotic color and unusual sonority to a contemporary program, and Wallingford Riegger's *Nonet for Brass*, Op. 49 (3231) is an eminently respectable twelve-tone, serial work — so difficult that one can almost use the individual parts as advanced contemporary etudes. This writer has yet to hear it accurately performed.

Brass Choir

The repertory of the brass choir really isn't good enough to justify a permanent concert ensemble, except in a conservatory or school of music where an ensemble based on the orchestral brass section can, if properly conducted, be an excellent vehicle for the training of professional players; or in a college or community orchestra where it might help solve the problem of what to do with the brass while the strings rehearse. But, although a regularly rehearsing brass choir is most likely to be found in a college or conservatory, an occasional ensemble to provide fanfares and ceremonial noises at special events is useful everywhere.

For an inexperienced high school group Leon Brown's arrangement of Purcell's (i.e. Clarke's) *Trumpet Voluntary* (4231-bar) is suitably festive for any occasion and the movie music in Clifford Barnes' *Robbins Collection of Music for Brass Choir* (3431-bar-timp-perc) is sure-fire stuff for unsophisticated players and audiences.

There is a rather large and varied group of moderately difficult works which are useful with college or very good high school players. For fanfares and ceremonial music Giovanni Gabrieli's *Canzon duodecimi toni* (2 x 2120/3020/2210-opt tba), Roger Smith's arrangement of the

Symphony from Act IV of Purcell's *The Fairy Queen* (6240/6060-timp-opt tba), Paul Dukas' *Fanfare pour précéder "La Péri"* (3431), Richard Arnell's *Ceremonial and Flourish* (3430), Thomas Beversdorf's *Cathedral Music* (3431-bar) and Aaron Copland's solemn *Fanfare for the Common Man* (3431-timp-perc) ought to provide something in almost any style for almost any occasion, sacred or secular. For a concert performance Walter Hartley's Sinfonia No. 3 (1963) (5431-bar); Herbert Haufrecht's conservative, richly scored Symphony (3431-timp); or Fisher Tull's colorful *Soundings* (6642-2bar-timp-perc) would be effective. A group rehearsing regularly should also investigate Robert King's *Seven Conversation Pieces* (4031-2bar), Leo Justinus Kauffmann's *Musik* (3431), John Hartmeyer's *Negev* (3331-bar-timp), Earl Zindars' *The Brass Square* (4431-timp-cym), Albert Cobine's *Vermont Suite* (4341-bar) and Paul Holmes's *Suite for Brass* (3431).

With a good college or conservatory ensemble Jacques Castérède's *Trois fanfares pour des proclamations de Napoléon* (3431-timp-perc-narrator) and Henri Tomasi's *Fanfares liturgiques* (3431-timp-perc) are long pieces for big events, and Debussy's fanfares from *Le Martyre de Saint-Sébastien* (4631-timp) and David Diamond's *Ceremonial Fanfare* (1950) (4631-timp-perc) are short pieces for smaller ones. Roy Jesson's *Variations and Scherzo* (4331-bar-timp-snare drum), James Marks's *Music for Brass and Timpani* (3431-bar-timp), Eino Rautavaara's *A Requiem in Our Time* (4431-bar-timp-perc) and Gardner Read's *Sound Piece, Op. 82* (4432-bar-timp-perc) are all effective and difficult concert numbers. Robert Beadell's *Introduction and Allegro* (3331-bar-timp), Usko Merilainen's *Partita for Brass* (4431), Thomas Merriman's *Theme and Four Variations* (4231-bar) and Wayne Scott's *Rondo giojoso* (3441-bar-timp-perc) are perhaps not quite as well written but they are still very suitable both for performance and study.

Chapter IV

Solos

If it is to be at all usable as a reference work, a book like this must be organized into what are, in reality, rather artificial chapters. A good teacher does not think simply of studies, duets, ensembles or solos, but of the combination of them that will be most effective in assuring the development of a particular aspect of technique or style. Nowhere does the inadequacy of a single-medium approach become more obvious than in this chapter on solos. Every good teacher treasures a small repertory of solos which are just the thing for solidifying or making relevant a specific point of instruction. Beyond this, the average school player of a brass instrument plays a solo in public perhaps a half-dozen times in his life — outside of state contest and church performances possibly not at all — so neither teacher nor student really has any need for a great arsenal of formal recital pieces. This is fortunate because, except for a few of the better pieces for horn, solos for brass instruments are a pretty sterile and artificial lot. Of course, if the repertory were better the student would probably be more likely to perform more often; it isn't, nor is it likely to improve a great deal.

With brass instruments it is very important that the solo repertory not be taken to mean the recital repertory. What could be less interesting, what could have less relevance to what is going on or has ever gone on in the real world of music, than a whole concert of music for trombone and piano, for example? Instead, teachers and students should be completely uninhibited in seeking out and using music of all periods, styles and media. A detailed discussion of this is, alas, beyond the scope of this book. However, a brief outline of some of the approaches open to the resourceful teacher is perhaps permissible. The junior high school is a good place for stirring up all kinds of quasi-informal concerts, recitals or whatever one wants to call them. These should be relaxed and varied, perhaps as part of the activity of a school chamber music club. The musical possibilities are virtually unlimited: folk songs with guitar and/or percussion accompaniment, pieces in jazz styles, a twelve-tone set composed by the student and played (and perhaps improvised upon) in its various permutations, chance music of all kinds, experiments with a tape recorder — all juxtaposed with more formal examples of Renaissance, Baroque or contemporary music. Whatever the shortcomings of our present musical era, many of its manifestations seem ideally suited to the activity of the adolescent (which may be just about where much of it belongs).

College students should roam the length and breadth of the library looking not for the music of obscure and deservedly forgotten *Kleinmeister* but for ways of inserting themselves into performances of first-rate works by first-rate composers. The ballades of Machaut, the motets of Lasso, the arias of Bach and the chamber music of Webern are but a few of the kinds of music that should appear on recitals given by trombonists and trumpeters. Let us hope that the stand-up recital for trumpet and piano has already become a relic of the past.

This sort of activity can be exhilarating and exciting, but it should not conceal for a moment the fact that all the resourcefulness in the world will not bring to the player of a brass instrument a repertory in any way comparable to those enjoyed by singers or string and keyboard players. For this reason players of brass instruments should early on be encouraged to double on an instrument chosen specifically for its breadth of repertory while not posing any conflict of embouchure — something like the violin, cello, piano or organ. (Or, if the student sings well, he should be encouraged to take voice lessons.) Brass instruments are fine when one is young and carefree, but they hardly lend dignity and richness to a graceful old age.

Trumpet Solos

Grade school children love to play what they know, and all the best-intentioned teaching solos in the world don't produce the practicing a good song book does. Send a child home with a nice book of folk songs or his classroom music book and you will be doing as well as anyone can. For a B-flat instrument and piano John Kinyon's *Breeze-Easy Recital Pieces* is a good grade-school collection. The tunes are familiar. The piano accompaniments are very spare, but if they seem a bit too thin just remember that the chances of finding someone who can play them are that much better. A more sophisticated collection is volume I of Sidney Lawton's *The Young Trumpet-Player*. Its little hymns, chorales and folk songs are especially good for youngsters who might want to play in Sunday School; and from a pedagogical standpoint they are excellent for working on a solid, clear tone. If the student still wants something with piano after he has become a little more fluent, one can try Lawrence Meyer's *Fifteen Folk Tunes*. The selection is less than inspired and the accompaniments do not always strike this writer as exactly appropriate, but it is something to play. Teachers who find such material both artificial and confining may want to start their students out reading in C rather than in B-flat. Then they are not dependent on a few published collections and can choose from a great variety of music — folk songs, hymns, almost anything.

Perhaps an even more sensible way out of both the accompaniment and the transposition problem is to use some of the little collections of unaccompanied tunes which are so abundantly available from the repertory of the soprano recorder. This writer's two favorites are Hans Bergese's *Alte und neue Tänze*[†] and Imogen Holst's *100 Traditional Irish Tunes*[†]. The Bergese is a collection of dances from the thirteenth through the twentieth century, published for recorder and hand drum. They are very attractive to young students, and their rhythmic sophistication and melodic freshness are delightful. The prefatory instructions are all in German, but the music itself needs no explanation; and if one wants to use the drum one need only remember that "F" is finger and "D" is thumb while looking at the diagram on page three, whereupon everything should be perfectly clear. The Holst is full of jigs, which are just the thing for prodding a hesitant student into playing faster, while the slower, more lyrical ballads provide pleasant and expressive contrast. There are no doubt dozens of similar and equally useful collections. Four more that work are Walter Frei's *Mittelalterliche Spielmannsmusik*[†], Medieval tunes for teachers and pupils tired of the "same old stuff"; Dietz Degen's *Fröhliche Jagd*[†], hunting calls which serve almost as well as Irish jigs for coaxing forth some added agility; Edgar Hunt's *Fifty Old English Folk-Dance Airs*[†]; and Willy Schneider's *Flötenbüchlein für einsame Spieler*[†], which has a bit of everything.

Finally, three contemporary suggestions: Warren Benson's *Prologue* is a sensitive first solo; George F. McKay's *Concert Solo Suite for*

Young Players is a laudable effort at writing a very easy piece for trumpet and piano that goes beyond the usual school music cliché's; and Karl Marx's *Flötenbüchlein für Klaus* (1950) is a volume of simple contemporary pieces for recorder and piano. For the Marx the pianist should play the accompaniment down an octave, since the recorder would sound an octave higher than written in the part, and the trumpeter must read in C.

*

There are several useful collections for young junior high school students. Volumes II and III of Lawton's *The Young Trumpet-Player* are full of very idiomatic arrangements of marches and trumpet tunes by Purcell, Handel, Clarke, Green, Stanley and Boyce — evoking, even for rather immature players, some of the elegant atmosphere of the trumpet's golden age. Willy Schneider's *Little Pieces by Old Masters* gathers up some fresh and trumpety arrangements of eighteenth-century pieces. The accompaniments are rather crude and heavy on the bass, and one suspects that some of the selections have been badly chopped up, but it is still one of the better collections. Clair Johnson's anthology of *Sacred Solos* is a bag of old chestnuts — Schubert's *Ave Maria,* Fearis's *Beautiful Isle of Somewhere,* Adam's *The Holy City,* etc. — but there is much to be said for them. More lovely cornet tone has probably evolved from *The Holy City* than from any other sixty-five measures in the repertory, and grandma is likely to love it. Daniel Canty's *Bugle Signals, Calls and Marches* is usually enthusiastically received by junior high school boys, in addition to being a valuable source of studies when a student is learning triple- and double-tonguing.

Additional eighteenth-century pieces for young students are most easily obtained by a little careful poaching in the soprano recorder's preserve. The parts are all in C, of course, but so much the better. Waldemar Woehl's arrangements of little *Spielstücke* from Johann Kaspar Ferdinand Fischer's *Le Journal de printemps* are a real find. They are short and trumpety, and even in C transposition many of them are not unduly high (*e''* or *f''* is a common top note). The accompaniments are very easy. Godfrey Finger's Sonata can be used as a more ambitious work by leaving off the last movement and perhaps transferring some of the melody to the keyboard instrument to give the trumpeter a chance to rest. James Hook's Sonata in G major is a nice recreational piece. Again one can transfer some of the melody to the keyboard part if necessary. Piano-playing mothers love it. In fact, any pianist who can play a Clementi Sonatina should be able to make the accompaniment sound reasonably fluent.

From the twentieth century Robert Sanders' syncopated, folksy bit of Americana, *Square Dance;* P. Cabus' lively, rhythmic *Rondo ostinato;* Georges Friboulet's wry, humorous *Introduction et marche;* R. Bernard Fitzgerald's idiomatically written but conservative English Suite and Alan Hovhaness's melismatic *Prayer of Saint Gregory* are good set pieces for a mature player. On the lighter side, Leroy Anderson's *A Trumpeter's Lullaby* is popular, and if the student likes this kind of music, more of the same can be found in a collection of his lesser-known numbers entitled *The Music of Leroy Anderson.* For strictly pedagogical purposes Vaclav Nelhybel's Suite is good for nit-picking. It is full of all kinds of fussy articulations and the student must develop a good eye for detail and a rather subtle command of staccato and accent to play the movements properly. Musically, however, it is very dull. From other repertories, the *Epigrams* from Zoltan Kodaly's *Choral Method* are good solfège training; Karl Fegers' *Acht Tanzmelodien* (1962) are nice little contemporary pieces, orginally for recorder and piano; and Konrad Lechner's *Volkslied-Improvisation*† is a very useful set of unaccompanied pieces, offering valuable practice in phrasing, a variety of rhythmic problems and some fairly wide intervals.

*

For skilled, older junior high players or for high school students who are coming along, Walter Eckard's *Twelve Program Solos* is a balanced, sophisticated selection of arrangements with well-written piano accompaniments. To continue the trumpeter's introduction to the styles and idioms of the eighteenth century, Georg Philipp Telemann's *Heldenmusik* is a useful set of short pieces which will not strain the embouchure very much, and Henry Coleman's arrangement of a *Trumpet Tune* by John Stanley is a good separate work from a slightly later period. Antonio Diabelli's Sonatina in C major, as arranged for recorder and piano, is good C transposition practice in a late and rather naive Classical style, and it is playable by a trumpeter with a sturdy high register and a pianist of only modest ability. One can always transfer a few phrases to the piano if the trumpet part is too strenuous, and the final high C's can be played an octave lower.

Recital pieces at this level are mostly what a colleague of the writer's calls "non-developmental." There are a number which are quite suitable for recreation or concert — in the unlikely event that the student has an accompanist and an opportunity to perform in a solo recital — but most of them are of limited pedagogical importance. Francis Findlay's arrangement of *Two Pieces* by Reinhold Glière presents two lovely compositions which require real sensitivity and flexibility, and bring out the best in fine young players. Quinto Maganini's adaptation of Prokofiev's *Kije's Wedding* is an apt choice, but repetitious. A little careful cutting might be wise. Morton Gould's *Pavanne,* as arranged by Michael Edwards, and Leroy Anderson's *Bugler's Holiday* are good light pieces. William Presser's Suite is gay and witty. The accompaniment is essential, but a high school pianist should be able to cope. As a serious chamber-music project for two players interested in contemporary music Lewis Raymond's *Design* is a good beginning. For best results it should be coached, rather than just left to the students to work out for themselves. Robert Clérisse's *Noce villageoise* and *Thème varié* are quite easy representatives of the French repertory. Clérisse's solos never look very interesting, but they often turn out to be more effective in a little concert than ones which at first appeared more attractive. Raymond Gallois Montbrun's *Lied* is very easy, sophisticated, and rather abstract. It is a good study for tone, but the accompaniment adds nothing. His *Marche* and *Scherzo* are agile and lively. The piano will never be missed. And as a sort of *pièce de resistance* at this level, and for really getting down to work on a true French style of playing, Pierre Gabaye's *Boutade* is very worthwhile.

*

With a high school student who plays very well, or a more-or-less average college student, Walter Beeler's *Solos for the Trumpet Player* is as usable a collection as any. It is quite a hodge-podge (arrangements of excerpts from eighteenth-century works, Balay's *Petite pièce concertante,* Adam's *Cantique de Noël,* etc.), but some teachers prefer collections to single editions, and this is indeed a collection. The editing of the eighteenth-century works is, to be sure, awful. To introduce a student to some original Baroque music for trumpet, Glasenapp and Wolf's compilation of anonymous movements entitled *Rostocker Suite* is easy and as interesting as one is likely to find.

There is also a lot of Baroque music which can be appropriated from other instruments. Woehl's edition for recorder and piano of some *Ausgewählte Menuette* by Telemann makes available some very nice, short pieces, several of which demand considerable accuracy and agility for their wide intervals. The accompaniment is very easy. Ernst Pätzold's selection of fifteen pieces from Telemann's *Sieben mal sieben und ein Menuett* for violin or woodwind is surprisingly varied, and the extreme angularity makes them valuable embouchure builders. In addition, they are fun to play and the accompaniment is not difficult. Johann Fischer's Suite in G major, as arranged for recorder and piano by Walter Bergmann, is very good for keeping the high register in trim without overdoing it. The range is fairly high (to b'') but the movements are compact. For a little change of pace, Colin Sterne's arrangement for recorder and piano of a Canzona by Girolamo Frescobaldi gives the student a chance to sample music of a somewhat earlier period. Two other publications which might be investigated are Willard Musser's adaptations of a sonata and a concerto (both originally for oboe) by Handel. Some students like this sort of thing, but alert teachers should point out that the editing of the phrasing and articulation is atrocious.

Johann Nepomuk Hummel's late-Classical Concerto is a popular showpiece for high school and college trumpeters, no doubt because trumpet music from this period is very scarce and because a band accompaniment is easily available. Arthur Frackenpohl's Sonatina based on sonatinas by Friedrich Kuhlau is a good warm-up for it. A couple of nineteenth-century (in style, at least) works which still make a bit of a smash are Alexander Goedicke's *Concert Etude*, Op. 49 and W. Brandt's *Concertpiece*, Op. 12. And no doubt one still can't write a chapter on music for the trumpet or cornet without mentioning that war horse of war horses, Arban's fantasy and variations on the *Carnival of Venice*.

If the student needs a formal recital piece, there are a number of works which are neither pretentious nor terribly difficult. Leonard Bernstein's rhythmic, staccato *Rondo for Lifey;* Walter Hartley's dissonant, quartal Sonatina; Richard Arnell's stylish *Trumpet allegro,* Op. 58, No. 2; Robert Starer's intense, chant-like *Invocation;* Jean Emanuel Aubain's suave, gallic *Marche et scherzo;* Hugo Cole's modern racetrack piece, *The Hammersmith Galop;* François Julien Brun's crisp and rather chromatic *Promenade;* and Günter Raphael's brilliant, quartal *Marche* are all vigorous and approachable, although somewhat lacking in contrast when regarded as a group. One needs something slow and sensitive to go along with them, like the two Glière-Findlay pieces mentioned earlier. If the trumpeter plays regularly with a pianist, four more suggestions for ensemble practice are Marius Flothuis's *Aria,* Op. 18 (1944); José Berghmans' *La Chenille;* Francis Baines' *Pastoral;* and a small collection entitled *Contemporary French Recital Pieces.* On the lighter side, Eddie Sauter's *Gershwin for Trumpet* has some nice period interpretations.

Students who have an opportunity to play in church will find Johann Ludwig Krebs's *Eight Chorale Preludes* and Harald Rohlig's *Eight Intradas and Chorales* worth bearing in mind. And if one happens to be in a nest of eggheads needing something for trumpet and orchestra there is Karl Breuer's atonal, serial *Atonalyse II.*

Unaccompanied solos are always extremely useful, but for some reason the trumpet is very badly served in this medium, unless one considers some of the better pieces from the etude repertory. Even the tuba is better off! At this stage only Heinz Schröter's *Fanfarette* seems worth recommending. To fill the void, trumpeters might investigate Jacob van Eyck's *Der Fluyten Lust-hof* — three fairly fat volumes of seventeenth-century psalm, dance and folksong variations — uncommonly useful pieces both for study (they are excellent transposition etudes for D trumpet) and recital.

*

The Baroque repertory is a tantalizing one for skilled college and conservatory players. The truth of the matter is that there are dozens of Baroque trumpet sonatas, almost all of them pieces only a musicologist could love. The archive of trumpet sonatas in Bologna, for example, is perhaps the most overrated collection of music anywhere, at least as far as yielding anything worth playing. The sonatas by Domenico Gabrielli are by far the best of the Bolognese repertory, and the six solo sonatas are now available in a modern edition for trumpet and piano, transposed down from D to C. Of the other Baroque sonatas currently published, the ones by Heinrich Biber, Alessandro Stradella and Henry Purcell are most likely to be of interest to the average player at this stage. Only the Purcell comes with a keyboard reduction. The little movements in Dietz Degen's edition for recorder and piano of Nicolaus Adam Strungk's *Suiten und Airs* are most worthwhile for familiarizing the student with the hemiola rhythms so frequent in the Stradella. Warren Roché's publication of twenty excerpts from Telemann's twelve Fantasias for unaccompanied flute is a nice idea, but it does not differ from the published edition for flute except in suggesting some lower-octave transpositions, and one can purchase the whole set of flute Fantasias, on better paper, for less. If one wants some early unaccompanied pieces to play, the van Eyck variations mentioned earlier will serve very well.

From the latter part of the eighteenth century there is, of course, Haydn's Concerto in E-flat major.

Of the smaller recital pieces, Iain Hamilton's dissonant *Capriccio;* Jacques Ibert's *Impromptu* (1951); Arthur Honegger's *Intrada;* Alun Hoddinott's nasty little *Rondo scherzoso;* Robert Oboussier's chromatic, angular *Entrada* (1943); Robert Blum's light, biting *Capriccio* (1959); Otto Ketting's improvisatory, unaccompanied *Intrada* (1958); Randell Croley's unaccompanied *Variazioni,* Op. 44, No. 3 (1965) and Barney Childs' *Interbalances IV* (1962), a chance piece for unaccompanied trumpet and optional narrator, are perhaps most likely to grace a program effectively. Additional unaccompanied solos can be found at the back of volume III of the Arban Maire *Méthode;* and some of the recent French etudes are of sufficient interest to be worth performing alone, notably several of the fifteen Etudes of Charles Chaynes. Among the larger accompanied works, William Mayer's *Concert Piece,* Henri Tomasi's *Triptyque,* Marius Constant's *Trois mouvements* and Henri Challan's Variations all merit at least a reading.

If the student can play regularly with a good accompanist, Hindemith's Sonata (1939) is an interesting project. If it is difficult to get a skilled pianist, Max Seeboth's Sonata and Viktor Korda's Sonatina can both be performed with student pianists of only moderate ability. Where ensemble coaching is part of the student's training, the sonatas by Halsey Stevens, Donald H. White, Karl Pilss (1935) and Boris Asafiev (1939) and the sonatina by Pierre Gabaye offer a wide range of stylistic and interpretative problems for both players. They are well worth undertaking as a group even though most of them are better study projects than concert works.

This writer regards nineteenth- and twentieth-century trumpet concertos, one and all, as ghastly. If the student has an opportunity to play with an orchestra he might do better to understate it a little by playing something like Enesco's *Legend* or Persichetti's *The Hollow*

Men. If one must play or study a concerto, Vittorio Giannini's and Wayne Bohrnstedt's are lively American ones. If one needs to put something together in a hurry, Knudage Riisager's Concertino, Op. 29 is good to keep in mind because the string parts are usually easy to get and it is not difficult to work up. The music is pretty awful, though. For a pops concert, Oskar Böhme's Concerto in F minor, Op. 18 is an old-fashioned and very tuneful virtuoso display piece, and Alexander Arutunian and Aleksandra Pakhmutova (1955) have written more recent works in the same tradition. Gaston Brenta's Concertino and Charles Chaynes' Concerto are French display pieces with a little bit of everything in them, while Pierre Lantier's Concerto is a short, fairly easy work in a more delicate French style. Hans Ahlgrimm's Concerto (1938) is a vigorous piece, fun to practice for an expansive, free-wheeling approach, but the accompaniment is comically old fashioned. John Addison's Concerto and Pierre Wissmer's Concertino (1959) are also worth investigating, although in almost any other repertory they wouldn't be.

*

For college or conservatory students of professional caliber, Telemann's Concerto in D major is a ripe Baroque work and Johann Melchior Molter's Concerto in D major represents Baroque clarino technique at its most advanced level (so advanced that some musicologists claim it was intended for clarinet, not trumpet). A pair of less distinguished but typical works are Johann Friedrich Fasch's Concerto in D major and Giuseppe Torelli's *Sinfonia con tromb*a. A challenging borrowing is Fritz Jöde's arrangement for recorder of several of Dietrich Buxtehude's *Choralvorspiele*. From the latter part of the eighteenth century, Johann Michael Haydn's Concerto in D major is a dignified but perilously high work; and Johann Georg Albrechtsberger's Concertino in E-flat major is a delicately textured, light piece which may well have been intended for jew's harp, believe it or not, but which is delightfully trumpety, nonetheless.

From the twentieth century, the sonatas by Kent Kennan and Harold Shapero (1940) are worth performing, while the sonatas by George Antheil and Victor Legley (1953) and the sonatinas by Jacques Castérède and Jean Françaix can profitably be studied for their various technical and stylistic problems. Jo van den Booren's *Game III* (1966) for trumpet and organ is one of the few really avant garde pieces in the trumpet's published repertory. And for trumpet and orchestra (or piano) Alfred Désenclos' *Incantation, Thrène et Danse;* Alain Weber's *Strophes* and Florent Schmitt's Suite, Op. 133 are all likely to be more rewarding than the concertos noted earlier in this chapter.

Horn Solos

Grade school horn students are no different from those on any other instrument. They like to play what they know. The song-book approach is more difficult here because the range of the melody is often either too high or too low. However, youngsters can have some fun and learn something at the same time playing familiar tunes by ear, starting on a convenient pitch, or copying them out in appropriate keys until they are ready to transpose directly from the printed page. If a pianist is available, John Kinyon's *Breeze-Easy Recital Pieces* are again useful because the melodies are well known and the accompaniments very easy; and Warren Benson's *Soliloquy,* Pierre Max Dubois' *A cor et a cri* and the second movement of Ruth Gipps' Sonatina, Op. 56 are pleasant and tuneful single pieces.

*

For junior high students a large and very nice collection of tasteful arrangements with moderately difficult piano accompaniments is to be found in between the exercises in F. Shollar's *Method for Horn.* It is rather a nuisance to lug around and out of print at the moment, but if a copy is available quite a few of them are worth Xeroxing out for one's intermediate pupils. A much-used series of arrangements is Vuillermoz's *Les Classiques du cor* — separately published settings of pieces by Bach, Grétry, Mendelssohn, etc. J. E. de Wolf's *Sonatine in oude stijl* is a completely derivative work in a pseudo-eighteenth-century idiom, but young hornists enjoy it and the second movement, a tuneful little *chasse,* is a perfect tonguing study. Reid Poole's *A Song of a City* is an above-average piece of school music, useful for coaxing forth a full, robust sound. Alexander Scriabine's *Romance* and Saint-Saëns' *Romance,* Op. 36 are mature but very easy, demanding a lovely, well-controlled tone. The Scriabine is coherent when practiced without the accompaniment, but the Saint-Saëns really needs the piano to make much sense. Robert Clérisse's *L'Absent* is a simple, old-fashioned French recital piece, Jeanine Rueff's *Cantilène* an aloof modern one and Jean Meyer's *Cordelinette* an easy but fairly long tone study.

*

High school or older junior high hornists will find a variety of challenging pieces in Mason Jones's *Solos for the Horn Player*. Among the separately published solos there is little that is good for introducing Baroque and Classical style except Michel Corrette's Concerto in C major, *"La Choisy"* — which, though rather dull, is useful practice for basic Baroque passagework — and Johann Michael Haydn's very interesting *Romance*. Trumpeters can fill this void with a number of pieces from the soprano recorder's ample repertory. Unfortunately these lie either too high or too low for horn. Teachers who want to be terribly clever can appropriate some of the really worthwhile ones like the *Spielstücke* from Johann Kaspar Ferdinand Fischer's *Le Journal de printemps*, directing the hornist to read the solo part in F and the pianist to transpose the accompaniment by adding a flat and reading the treble clef as mezzo-soprano clef an octave higher and the bass clef as soprano clef an octave lower. Don't panic. It's not as difficult as it sounds and it would seem a very useful skill for anyone who has much to do with young horn players.

The twentieth-century repertory for young hornists is both varied and useful. There is a pretty little recital group in Alexander Glazunov's *Reverie*, Op. 24; Reinhold Glière's *Nocturne*, Op. 35, No. 10 and *Intermezzo*, Op. 35, No. 11; and A. Piguet's arrangement of Ravel's *Pavane pour une infante défunte*. (There is also an arrangement of the Ravel in Jones's *Solos for the Horn Player*.) Jean Françaix's *Canon in octave* provides some vigorous contrast to these and, properly taught, a good introduction to uninhibited French style as well. Frank Levy's Suite is an excellent teaching piece for many basic aspects of style, interpretation and technique — and young students like it. Paul Whear's *Pastorale Lament* and Feodor Akimenko's *Melody* are pleasant tone studies if the pupil has a good high *a''*. Neil Butterworth's *Prelude and Scherzo* is a conservative contemporary work with a fairly easy accompaniment. Two high school students should have no difficulty working it up. Halsey Stevens' *Four Short Pieces* are rather vague but in an idiom more dissonant and less cloying than usual; and they, too, could be played by two high school students of modest ability. Czeslaw Grudzinski's *Miniatury* might have some usefulness as studies, but the accompaniment is at times ludicrously overblown.

*

For very good high school players or college students without a great deal of experience, F. A. Rosetti's Concerto in E-flat major is an excellent introduction to the horn's all-too-limited stock of worthwhile Classical concertos. Just as there are dozens of Baroque trumpet sonatas which simply are not worth anyone's time, so there are dozens of Classical horn concertos which are just plain boring. However, this particular Rosetti concerto is quite tuneful and pleasant to practice, and it manages to touch on most of the problems common to horn concertos of the period, notably some of the ubiquitous *batteries de second cor*. From the nineteenth-century repertory a player with a lot of conventional technique would probably enjoy rattling away at Franz Strauss's lusty and rather naive Theme and Variations, Op. 13. Joseph Jongen's *Lied* provides something a little calmer.

Eugene Weigel's *Maine Sketches* and Natalie Tillotson's *Fantasy* (1959) are mature, interesting, twentieth-century recital pieces; and Leonard Bernstein's *Elegy for Mippy I*, Donald R. Jones's *Allegro*, Paul Holmes's *Serenade*, Robin Orr's *Serenade*, Arnold Cooke's Rondo in B-flat and Henri Tomasi's *Danse profane* are all worth at least a reading. From the unaccompanied repertory Egon Wellesz's *Fanfares*, Op. 78 are useful studies for agility and flexibility; and Bernhard Krol's *Laudatio* is a somewhat unusual vehicle for displaying or developing a full, affirmative style.

*

College is the time for the four Mozart Concertos, although most players will have studied them long before. This is a pity, really. Among Classical concertos in general they are very minor works, and what charm they possess comes in large measure from being played with ease and elegance — something few high school (or, for that matter, college) hornists are able to do. If the repertory of the Classical horn concerto is generally undistinguished, the repertory of the Classical horn sonata is virtually non-existent. Franz Danzi's Sonata in E-flat major, Op. 28 is one of the rare ones — more fun for the pianist than for the hornist and not very rewarding for either. As healthy Baroque exercise hornists might look into the seventeenth-century psalm, dance

and folksong variations in Jacob van Eyck's *Der Fluyten Lust-hof,*
published for unaccompanied recorder. (These are also very useful
for transposition studies — up or down.)

From the nineteenth century Richard Strauss's Concerto No. 1, Op.
11 is another work which should be played easily or not at all (which
at least is more than can be said for his Concerto No. 2); and the
second of Cherubini's two Sonatas (originally and more appropriately
entitled Etudes) is a worthwhile study for typical turn-of-the nineteenth-
century passagework.

There are a number of good, short, twentieth-century recital pieces,
of which Francis Poulenc's *Elégie* (1957), Carl Nielsen's *Canto serioso,*
Emmanuel Chabrier's *Larghetto,* Iain Hamilton's *Aria,* Arthur Butterworth's *Romanza* and William Presser's *Fantasy on the Hymn Tune
"The Mouldering Vine"* are a representative selection. The Chabrier
can also be played with orchestra or in an interesting arrangement for
horn and woodwind ensemble (which should be slightly re-edited from
the original before performing), the Butterworth, with a string quartet.
Two useful teaching solos are O. Miroshnikov's *Rondo,* for jaunty,
accurate staccato technique; and Eugène Bozza's *Chant lointain,* for
uninhibited French style. From the chamber music repertory Heinz
Schreiter's Sonatine, Op. 12; Hindemith's Sonata (1943) for alto horn;
and Bernhard Heiden's Sonata (1939) are fine study and recital
projects. Mark Hughes' Sonata is useful to know about if one must
play a long program because it gives the hornist plenty of rest. Hans
Poser's Sonata, Op. 8 is something else to play, but too repetitious for
concert performance.

*

Advanced college or conservatory players will find Telemann's Concerto in D major a typical but rather tedious excursion into the realm
of the Baroque horn concerto. It is not a first-rate piece, but it is one
of the few published examples of the genre — not that any of the
unpublished ones are likely to be much better. From the latter part
of the century the two concertos attributed to Franz Joseph Haydn;
Mozart's *Concert Rondo* and Peter Hogdson's arrangement for horn
and piano of his Horn Quintet, K. 407; Rosetti's Concerto in D
minor and Adam Gottron's telescoped edition of two concertos by
Johann Wenzel Stich (the famous Punto) which he calls Concerto No.
7 will all contribute to the development of the student's Classical
technique. Several other concertos by Rosetti and Stich have recently

been reprinted, but more impoverished works can hardly be imagined. Perhaps the most sensible thing to do with them is to keep a music notebook, enter in it the various batteries de second cor which are their only real challenge, and simply forget the rest (which is not hard to do). Like most Classical sonatas for a wind instrument and piano, Beethoven's Op. 17 is more fun for the pianist than for the hornist, and it was probably intended more to enliven a piano recital than anything else, but hornists ought to perform it at least once during the course of their studies. Franz Danzi's Sonata concertante, Op. 44 is of the same genre, but as approached by a composer with only mediocre talent.

Of the nineteenth-century pieces, Schumann's *Adagio und allegro,* Op. 70 is robust and impassioned but very difficult; and Joseph Rheinberger's Sonata in E-flat major, Op. 178 is, like the Beethoven, primarily a pianist's piece. Two other oft-cited works, Rossini's *Prelude, thème et variations* and von Weber's Concertino in E minor, Op. 45 are a pair of musical horrors — likely candidates for the music notebook but little more.

From the twentieth century Hindemith's Sonata (1939); Niels Viggo Bentzon's Sonata, Op. 47 and Quincy Porter's Sonata are respectable on any recital program. Helmut Eder's Sonatine, Op. 34, No. 6 is a worthwhile project, especially for problems of rhythmic ensemble. The sonatas by Robert Sanders (1958), Anthony Donato, Halscy Stevens, Peter Jona Korn and Leslie Bassett; Verne Reynolds' Partita; and Christian Wolff's avant garde *Duet II* all merit study if the hornist plays regularly with a pianist, and especially if they receive some systematic coaching. A shorter recital piece, Pierre Capdevielle's *Elégie de Duino,* is a fine etude and a veritable catalogue of twentieth-century problems and techniques.

Of the unaccompanied works Hans Erich Apostel's Sonatina, Op. 39b is an austere serial piece; William Presser's *Three Pieces* (1966) a difficult and rather obvious quodlibet; Barney Childs' *Variations for David Racusen* an atonal anthology of horn style and M. Camargo Guarnieri's *Etude* (1953) a good legato study. Otto Ketting's *Intrada* (1958) for unaccompanied trumpet or horn is relentlessly high for horn, although there probably is no reason why it couldn't be transposed. Down a third or so it could be a good recital opener or warm-up. There are also a number of interesting etudes which can be used as unaccompanied solos, notably No. 2 of Bozza's *18 Etudes* (1961);

Nos. 3 and 12 of Alain Weber's *13 Etudes* (1959); Nos. 5, 7, 9-11 and 13-15 of Charles Chaynes' *15 Etudes* (1959); Nos. 1-5, 7 and 10-12 of Marcel Bitsch's *12 Etudes* (1959); and Nos. 3, 6, 10, 12, 15-16, 18, 22 and 44 of Verne Reynolds' *48 Etudes* (1961).

To perform with an orchestra, Hindemith's Concerto (1949) and Paul Dukas' *Villanelle* are obvious choices; Reinhold Glière's Concerto, Op. 91 is long, old-fashioned and heroic; and Robert Kurka's *Ballad,* Op. 36 and Armin Schibler's *Prologue, Invocation et Danse,* Op. 47 are lesser-known, shorter works. Finally, Florent Schmitt's *Lied et scherzo,* Op. 54 for horn and double wind quintet is worth bearing in mind for a wind ensemble program.

Trombone Solos

For grade school players John Kinyon's *Breeze-Easy Recital Pieces* is again useful for its familiar tunes and simple accompaniments; Alfred Moffat's *Old Masters for Young Players,* a standard volume for beginning cellists, makes available a number of very easy arrangements of Baroque and Classical pieces, of which several lie very well for trombone; and Warren Benson's *Aubade* is a tasteful, separately published solo.

*

At the junior high level Gene Mullins' *Twelve Easy Classics* is a nice collection with useful pieces for working on a full tone and a lyrical style, but they require a firm high register up to and including *a'*. If these are too high, Moffat's *Old Master Melodies for Young Cellists* has many attractive eighteenth-century tunes which are also idiomatic for trombone, and they do not go above *d'*. There are also a couple of very suitable arrangements in the Russian collection of *Six Pieces* by Gretchaninov *et al* for bassoon and piano. This particular publication is now out of print, but it is the sort of thing one keeps an eye out for when one teaches youngsters. John J. Morrissey's *Song for Trombone* is a musical blank, but it is something easy to play and it has an accompaniment for band. François Daneels' *Petite pièce* is equally undistinguished, but it is simple and tuneful to practice, and the student must play affirmatively to make it sound like anything at all.

*

For better junior high or middling high school students who still need rather easy material, Henri Gagnebin's *Sarabande* is a mature, well-constructed recital piece, playable in the best of company. Robert Clérisse's *Prière* is especially good solfège practice in a simple piece which two high school players should be able to put together on their own. Robert Bariller's *L'Enterrement de Saint-Jean* is useful for working on a robust tone. Paul Tanner's *Moods from Dorian* is an excellent study for several basic rhythmic patterns, tone and breath control. The accompaniment never will be missed.

*

Teachers of high school students often find Henry C. Smith's *Solos for the Trombone Player* a useful collection, but this writer can't get very excited about it, mainly because so many of the selections are excerpts at a time when most students should be past the excerpt stage. Harold Perry's *Classical Album* is an anthology of smaller pieces, set very high for the trombone. They lie in a lovely range (*b♭* to *b♭'*) and offer valuable high register work for a very fine student, but less well-endowed pupils will be completely frustrated by them. Thomas Beversdorf's group of transcriptions of arias by Bach, Handel and Haydn is exceptionally useful from a pedagogical point of view, providing practice in interpretation, fluent legato tone and technique, and tenor clef. One can also use them as vehicles for the study of eighteenth-century articulation patterns (to which the slurs provided have very little relevance).

Among the more-or-less contemporary works, Roger Boutry's *Choral varié* and Henri Tomasi's *Danse sacrée* are good French recital pieces, fine for displaying a full, solid tone. The Tomasi isn't very practical unless the student plays often with a pianist, however, because the trombone part makes little sense by itself. Vladislav Blazhevich's *Concert Sketch No. 5* is a nice piece for a studio recital, demanding a varied blend of tone and modest technique. Pierre Max Dubois' *Deux marches* and his *Cortège* are useful for cultivating a lusty French style, and they are reasonably coherent when practiced without the accompaniment. Both of the marches ascend to *c''*, but in short passages which can easily be edited out if this is too high. Pierre Gabaye's *Tubabillage* is lively and tuneful, with a modest tessitura, — a worthwhile study for bass trombone or for that stuffy register from *c* to *g*. Jirí Pauer's *Capricci* for bassoon and piano is a pleasant series of short, contrasting movements, playable on trombone with very little adaptation, and especially good for light, staccato playing.

*

Very good high school or inexperienced college students can find a wealth of interesting material among the Baroque cello and bassoon sonatas. Luidgi Merci's bassoon Sonata in G minor, Op. 3, No. 4 is a nice one to start with, and Willem de Fesch's six cello Sonatas, Op. 8 provide much pleasant and useful music. Johann Ernst Galliard's bassoon sonatas are often played and they do offer a lot of practice in quick, angular passages, although they are actually among the least interesting of the Baroque sonatas. Giuseppe Torelli's cello Sonata in G major, Domenico dalla Bella's cello Sonata in C major, Filippo Banner's cello Sonata in G minor and Michel Corrette's bassoon Sonata in D minor, Op. 20, No. 2 are all directly playable by trombonists and are very useful for working on a quick, light technique and on eighteenth-century performance practice problems like improvisation, ornamentation and articulation.

Alas, the trombone's own stock of nineteenth- and twentieth-century pieces isn't nearly as interesting at this level. From the French repertory Alexandre Guilmant's *Concertpiece,* Op. 88 is standard Romantic recital fare and Théodore Dubois' *Concertpiece* is a less interesting work of the same vintage. J. E. Barat's *Andante et allegro* is a light, idiomatic representative of the older twentieth-century French contest solos. Robert Bariller's *Hans de Schnokeloch* is a tuneful piece for bass trombone — puerile but pleasant. William Presser's Sonatina isn't very serious but it is fun to play and could be worked on as an ensemble project by two players of modest ability. Rimsky-Korsakov's Concerto for trombone and band is lyrical but otherwise undistinguished, and Alan Hovaness's Concerto No. 3; *Diran (The Religious Singer)* for baritone horn and string orchestra is equally idiomatic for trombone and easy enough for most high school orchestras.

*

For good college students there are several suitable cello sonatas, like Johann Christoph Friedrich Bach's Sonata in G major or de Fesch's expressive Sonata in D minor, Op. 13, No. 4, which make fine recital pieces for trombone. Others, like the six sonatas of Benedetto Marcello or Felice Maria Picinetti's Sonata in C major are perhaps best reserved for recreation or study, where the Picinetti offers especially valuable practice toward a light, loose technique. From the repertory of the unaccompanied recorder the miscellaneous variations in Jacob van Eyck's *Der Fluyten Lust-hof* (treble clef) provide an enormous amount of material for developing various aspects of early Baroque technique and performance practice. There are also several eighteenth-century bassoon concertos which skilled players might find diverting. From the early part of the century, Johann Wilhelm Hertel's Concerto in A minor is a rousing, pre-Classical piece; and from the latter half, Johann Christian Bach's Concerto in E-flat major, Carl Stamitz's Concerto in F major and Franz Danzi's Concerto in F major are very good, albeit a bit dry — more or less playable by intrepid trombonists.

From the nineteenth century at least two concertos are still in the repertory, robust examples of a time in which the trombone was surprisingly popular: Ferdinand David's Concertino, Op. 4 and Friedebald Gräfe's Concerto.

Of the twentieth-century recital pieces Carlos Salzedo's *Pièce concertante,* Op. 27 is a lilting, melodious work in an older French style and Boutry's *Capriccio* requires the proper *élan* of the modern French idiom. Otto Henry's neo-Baroque *Passacaglia and Fugue* and Jacques Castérède's *Fantaisie concertante* are good study or concert pieces for bass trombone and piano. Somehow the trombone seems to attract pieces which look tantalizingly easy but which are difficult to make much sense of, like Bennie Beach's Suite, Arthur Frackenpohl's *Pastorale,* John Gardner's *Romanza* and Wilfred Mellers' *Galliard.* They are perhaps worth investigating if one needs a rather easy but sophisticated work.

In the chamber music department Klaus George Roy's Sonata, Op. 13 is an effective and not very difficult mainstream contemporary work which would be a worthwhile project, either for recital or simply for study. Castérède's Sonatina is a robust French piece. John Boda's energetic Sonatina (1954), R. R. Trevarthen's Sonata and Walter Watson's blander, more conservative Sonatina are all easy to put together; and Robert Schollum's more abstract Sonatina for bassoon and piano, Op. 55, No. 3 (1956) can be played on trombone as a challenging study for rhythmic coordination.

*

Fine college or conservatory players should continue to enrich their repertory of Baroque and Classical works with music originally intended for cello and bassoon. Vivaldi's cello sonatas are obvious choices in this respect, and sophisticated players will want to use the Kolneder edition of the cello sonatas themselves, instead of the editions especially adapted for trombone, because the editing is so much more reliable. Johann Friedrich Fasch's bassoon Sonata in C major (also published in an acceptable edition for trombone) is a ripe and difficult Baroque showpiece, and J.C.F. Bach's cello Sonata in A major is a worthy representative of a somewhat later style. From the concerto literature Johann Georg Albrechtsberger's Concerto in B-flat major and Georg Christoph Wagenseil's Concerto in E-flat major are interesting curiosities from an era when the trombone was much more prominent than is generally realized. Both were intended for alto trombone and the tessitura is high. On the other hand, eighteenth-century bassoon concertos rarely go above *a'* for the soloist and, although they tend to have a lot of wide skips and angular passagework, whatever endurance problems they have come from length, not height. Johann Christian Bach's bassoon Concerto in B-flat major is one of the better ones — a good-humored work full of fluffy passagework and wide leaps. Trombonists may not want to use it on a formal concert, but it is a very pleasant way to practice.

Of the twentieth-century recital pieces, André Ameller's *Kryptos* is a difficult atonal work; Rolf Looser's *Variationenfantasie* is heavy and somber; and Georges Hugon's *Introduction et allegro* and Alfred Désenclos' *Plain-chant et allegretto* are typical of the more difficult French works.

There is a steadily growing and very challenging repertory of music for unaccompanied trombone. Leonard Bernstein's *Elegy for Mippy II* is a useful short recital piece. Fritz Reuter's neo-Baroque Suite, Op. 23 is an older work, too long to be played all at once on a recital, but a good study for many conventional problems. Leslie Bassett's Suite; John Bavicchi's *Preludes,* Op. 21 and Roger Boutry's Concertino (at the back of his *12 Etudes de haut perfectionnement*) are difficult, angular and abstract — suitable both for study and performance. Barney Childs' part tinker-toy Sonata (1961) and John Cage's *Solo for Sliding Trombone* (1957-58) view the world from much farter out. For bass trombonists several of the "*10* (i.e. *12*) *Etudes modernes*" at the back of Paul Bernard's *Méthode* and Randell Croley's

Variazioni piccola (sic), Op. 44, No. 1 can be used for recital as well as study.

Of the more difficult accompanied sonatas, Paul Hindemith's Sonata (1941) and Walter Hartley's Sonata concertante (1956-58) are consistently interesting; and Robert Sanders' Sonata in E-flat major, Leslie Bassett's Sonata and Robert W. Jones's Sonatina are other worthwhile ensemble projects. Robert Schollum's Sonatina for bassoon and piano, Op. 57, No. 3 (1961) is a really crunchy practice piece *(en duo)* for rhythmic and melodic accuracy.

From the works with orchestra Darius Milhaud's spirited *Concertino d'hiver* (1953) for trombone and strings is very effective and the parts can be purchased. Of the other French concertos, Roger Boutry's is perhaps the most usable, but better as an etude than as a concert work. Jules Semler-Collery's *Fantaisie lyrique* is an expansive display piece, and Paul Creston's *Fantasy,* Op. 42 is long and high. Armin Schibler's *Signal, Beschwörung und Tanz,* Op. 55 and Frank Martin's *Ballade* (1940) are more abstract and not particularly attractive to many players and audiences. For trombone and band Wilson Coker's Concerto for tenor-bass trombone and symphonic band is a very angular, difficult work — not the sort of thing one usually associates with band concerts and probably more likely to be used as a study.

Tuba Solos

No one ever claimed that the tuba had any solo repertory; and for this reason, if for no other, one should think twice before consigning anyone to the tuba player's fate. Besides, the combination of tuba and piano is sheer madness. Tuba players play with piano like lemmings march to the sea, out of blind, suicidal tradition. Nobody wants to be left out.

John Kinyon's *Breeze-Easy Recital Pieces* are as good as any for starting our little lemming on his merry march, and for an intermediate student Harry I. Phillips' set of *Eight bel canto Songs* is a fine idea for developing tone and legato playing (something young tuba players rarely master). It is with real regret that the writer must report that the publisher's price — five dollars for eight little songs — is a scandal. As separate solos Warren Benson's *Arioso* is tasteful and very easy, and Bennie Beach's *Lamento* is useful for an older, sophisticated student. It has no technical difficulties except for a short, angular, legato passage which might be cut and which is very good to practice.

For a high school student Herbert Wekselblatt's *Solos for the Tuba Player* is the poorest of the Schirmer series, with only one or two really usable selections. James Christensen's *Ballad* is possible as a legato study, George F. McKay's *Suite for Bass Clef Instruments* is better-than-average school music and William Presser's *Rondo* is an amusing light recital piece.

For a college or very good high school player William Schmidt's Serenade, Walter Hartley's Sonatina (1957), his Suite for unaccompanied tuba, and John Diercks' *Variations on a Theme of Gottschalk* are proper recital pieces; and Paul Holmes' *Lento* and Robert Spillman's *Two Songs* qualify as "the best of the rest." The tessitura of the Spillman is very high.

At the college or conservatory level Halsey Stevens' Sonatina (1959-60) is a first-rate ensemble project with difficult problems of rhythmic coordination. Paul Hindemith's Sonata (1943), Thomas Beversdorf's Sonata (1956), Hartley's Sonata (1967), Jenö Takacs's *Sonata capricciosa,* Op. 81 and Merle Hogg's Sonatina are all worthy of performance and study. Vincent Persichetti's Serenade No. 12, Op. 88 and Presser's Suite are useful unaccompanied numbers. Leonard Bernstein's *Waltz for Mippy III* is a short, slight recital piece. The original, separately published version is very high. The version in the Wekselblatt collection has most of the tuba part transposed down an octave, although the piano part is unchanged. The concertos by Ralph Vaughan Williams and Robert Spillman also lie very high — and neither is really worth playing.

Chapter V

Books and Articles about Brass Instruments

There are two books about brass instruments which every instrumental music teacher should have in his library and at least one more which he should have read before beginning to teach: Philip Farkas's *The Art of Brass Playing*, R. Morley Pegge's *The French Horn* and Rafael Méndez's *Prelude to Brass Playing*. The Farkas includes a very sensible discussion of the embouchure which should be studied thoroughly by anyone teaching brass instruments. It is an exceptionally well illustrated volume, and at lesson time the pictures alone are worth the price. There is at present no good general book on the history of brass instruments, and in its absence the Morley Pegge provides the most useful information. Since the trombone really hasn't changed for centuries, and since, like the horn, the trumpet's main evolution has centered around the development and application of the valve, a volume on the history of the horn is not as limited as it might first appear. The Méndez is written in an unfortunately juvenile style, yet it reminds one more forcefully than any other book of the importance of laying a careful and proper foundation of good embouchure development at the very start of one's teaching.

For teachers wanting more specialized information of various kinds the articles on brass instruments in the fifth edition of *Grove's Dictionary of Music and Musicians* are generally very good, as are those in the old eleventh edition (1911) of the *Encyclopaedia Britannica*. The bibliographies following the articles on brass instruments in *Die Musik in Geschichte und Gegenwart* are useful for quick reference, while the ones in the "Brass Bibliography" series in *Brass Quarterly* (1957-1964) are more exhaustive. Numerous interesting small historical articles can be found in the various issues of *The Galpin Society Journal* (1948-   ), *Brass Quarterly* and *Brass and Woodwind Quar-*

terly (1966-   ); and an occasional worthwhile pedagogical article turns up among the generally puerile offerings of *The Instrumentalist*.

The horn is the subject of three other useful books: Farkas's *The Art of Horn Playing,* Robin Gregory's *The Horn* and Gunther Schuller's *Horn Technique.* Mr. Farkas's book is very practical and well illustrated, and it is especially good to use with talented high school students who are unable to study with a professional hornist. Messrs. Gregory and Schuller address themselves more to fellow hornists wanting to know more about their instruments, although the books are also very useful for non-hornists (conductors, composers, etc.) wanting to understand what makes horn players tick.

Although belonging to otherwise excellent series, Philip Bates' *The Trumpet and Trombone* and Edward Kleinhammer's *The Art of Trombone Playing* aren't very satisfactory.

BIBLIOGRAPHY

Abbreviations:

ML   Music and Letters
MMR   Monthly Musical Record
MT   Musical Times
PRMA   Proceedings of the Royal Musical Association

Brass Instruments — History and Literature

Articles in Lavignac-La Laurencie, *Encyclopédie de la musique et dictionnaire du Conservatoire*. Paris, Delagrave 1913-1931. 2. ptie. vol. 3 (1927):
Franquin, M. J. B. "La Trompette et le cornet," 1597-1637.
Flandrin, G. P. A. L. "Le Trombone." 1649-1659.
Arnold, Denis. "Ceremonial Music in Venice at the Time of the Gabrielis." *PRMA* 82 (1955/56) 47-59.
Balmert, Heinz, T. Herzberg and Herbert Schramm. *Metallblasinstrumente*. Leipzig, Fachbuchverlag 1958. 254 p.
Bate, Philip. *The Trumpet and Trombone*. London, E. Benn; New York, W. W. Norton 1966. 272 p.
Brass Quarterly. Durham, New Hampshire 1957-64. 7 vols.
Brass and Woodwind Quarterly. Durham, New Hampshire 1966- . irregular
Ehmann, Wilhelm. *Tibilustrium. Das geistliche Blasen, Formen und Reformen*. Kassel, Bärenreiter 1950. 174 p.
The Galpin Society Journal. n.p. 1948-.   annual
Jahn, Fritz. "Die Nürnberger Trompeten- und Posaunenmacher im 16. Jahrhundert." *Archiv für Musikwissenschaft* 7 (1925) 23-52.
Karstädt, Georg. "Zur Geschichte des Zinken und seiner Verwendung in der Musik des 16. bis 18. Jahrhunderts." *Archiv für Musikforschung* 2 (1937) 385-432.
Kingdon-Ward, Martha. "In Defense of the Ophicleide." *MMR* 82 (1952) 199-205.
Mahrenholz, C. "Ueber Posaunenmusik." *Musik und Kirche* 1 (1929) 132-137, 163-173, 261-267.
Russell, John F. and J. H. Elliot. *The Brass Band Movement*. London, J.M. Dent 1936. 240 p.
Squire, W. Barclay. "Purcell's Music for the Funeral of Mary II." *Sammelbände der Internationalen Musikgesellschaft* 4 (1902/03) 225-233.
Worthmüller, Willi. Die Instrumente der Nürnberger Trompeten- und Posaunenmacher. In: *Mitteilungen des Vereins für Geschichte der Stadt Nürnberg* (1955) 372-480.
————. Die Nürnberger Trompeten- und Posaunenmacher des 17. und 18. Jahrhunderts. as above (1954) 208-325.

Trumpet — History and Literature

Blandford, W. F. H. "The 'Bach Trumpet'." *MMR* 65 (1935) 49-51, 73-76, 97-100.

Cudworth, C. "Some New Facts About the Trumpet Voluntary." *MT* 94 (1953) 401-403.

Cudworth, C. and F. Zimmerman. "The Trumpet Voluntary." *ML* 41 (1960) 342-348.

Kolneder, Walter. "Il Concerto per due trombe di Antonio Vivaldi." *Rivista Musicale Italiana* 55 (1953) 54-63.

Osthoff, Wolfgang. "Trombe sordine." *Archiv für Musikwissenschaft* 13 (1956) 77-95.

Sachs, Curt. "Chromatic Trumpets in the Renaissance." *Musical Quarterly* 36 (1950) 62-66.

Tilmouth, Michael. "Corelli's Trumpet Sonata." *MMR* 90 (1960) 217-221.

Horn — History and Literature

Blandford, W. F. H. "Studies on the Horn, No. 1: The French Horn in England." *MT* 63 (1922) 544-547.

Coar, Birchard. *The French Horn.* De Kalb, Ill., The Author 1947. 102 p.

————. *A Critical Study of the Nineteenth-Century Horn Virtuosi in France.* De Kalb, Ill., The Author 1952. 168 p.

Gregory, Robin. "The Horn in Beethoven's Symphonies." *ML* 33 (1952) 303-310.

Halfpenny, Eric. "Tantivy: an Exposition of the 'Ancient Hunting Notes'." *PRMA* 80 (1953/54) 43-58.

Karstädt, Georg. *Lass lustig die Hörner erschallen! Fine kleine Kulturgeschichte der Jagdmusik.* Hamburg and Berlin, P. Parey 1964. 136 p.

Kingdon-Ward, Martha. "Mozart and the Horn." *ML* 31 (1950) 318-332.

Morley Pegge, R. *The French Horn.* London, E. Benn; New York, Philosophical Library 1960. 222 p.

Piersig, F. *Die Einführung des Hornes in die Kunstmusik und seine Verwendung bis zum Tode J. S. Bachs.* Halle, Niemeyer 1927. 146 p.

Ringer, Alexander. "The Chasse as a Musical Topic of the 18th Century." *Journal of the American Musicological Society* 6 (1953) 148-159.

Shone, A. B. "Coaching Calls." *MT* 92 (1951) 256-259.

Taut, Kurt. *Beiträge zur Geschichte der Jagdmusik.* Leipzig, Radelli & Hille 1927. 190 p.

Trombone — History and Literature

Besseler, Heinrich. "Die Entstehung der Posaune." *Acta Musicologica* 22 (1950) 8-35.

Galpin, F. W. "The Sackbut, its Evolution and History." *PRMA* 33 (1906/07) 1-25.

Maurer, Joseph A. "The Moravian Trombone Choir." *The Historical Review of Berks County* 20 (Oct.-Dec. 1954) 2-8.

Biography

Bridges, Glenn. *Pioneers in Brass.* Detroit, Mich., Sherwood Publications 1965. 113 p.

Clarke, Herbert L. *How I Became a Cornetist; The Autobiography of a Cornet-Playing Pilgrim's Progress.* St. Louis, J. L. Huber 1934. 74 p.

Schering, Arnold. "Zu Gottfried Reiches Leben und Kunst." *Bach Jahrbuch* 15 (1918) 133-140.

Werner, Arno. "Johann Ernst Altenburg, der letzte Vertreter der heroischen Trompeter- und Paukerkunst." *Zeitschrift für Musikwissenschaft* 15 (1932/33) 258-274.

Brass Instruments — Study and Teaching

Cheney, Edward A. "Adaptation to Embouchure as a Function of Dento-Facial Complex." *American Journal of Orthodontics* 35 (June 1949) 440-443.

Cheney, Edward A. and Byron O. Hughes. "Dento-Facial Irregularity — How it Influences Wind Instrument Embouchure." *Etude* 64 (1946) 379+, 439-440, 499-500.

Ehmann, Wilhelm. *Bläser-Fibel.* Kassel, Bärenreiter 1955, 1962. 2 vols: 88, 46 p.

Farkas, Philip. *The Art of Brass Playing.* Bloomington, Ind., Brass Publications 1962. 65 p.

Hofmann, Heinrich. *Ueber den Ansatz der Blechbläser.* Kassel, Bärenreiter 1956. 77 p.

Méndez, Rafael. *Prelude to Brass Playing.* New York, C. Fischer 1961. 123 p.

Porter, Maurice M. *The Embouchure.* London, Boosey & Hawkes 1967. 144 p.

Reinhardt, Donald S. *The Encyclopedia of the Pivot System.* New York, C. Colin 1964. 237 p.

Trumpet — Study and Teaching

Bush, Irving R. *Artistic Trumpet Technique and Study.* Hollywood, Calif., Highland Music Co. 1962. 96 p.

Dale, Delbert A. *Trumpet Technique.* London, Oxford Univ. Press 1965. 93 p.

Horn — Study and Teaching

Farkas, Philip. *The Art of French Horn Playing.* Evanston, Ill., Summy-Birchard 1956. 95 p.

Gregory, Robin. *The Horn.* London, Faber and Faber 1961. 250 p.

Moore, Paul B. *French Horn Valve Care.* Univ. of Portland (Ore.) Press 1965. 40 p.

Schuller, Gunther. *Horn Technique.* London, Oxford Univ. Press 1962. 118 p.

Trombone — Study and Teaching

Kleinhammer, Edward. *The Art of Trombone Playing.* Evanston, Ill., Summy-Birchard 1963. 107 p.

Bibliography

TRUMPET METHODS AND STUDIES

Arban, J. J. B. L. Famous Complete Trumpet, Cornet and Saxhorn Method. New edition in three parts, entirely revised in accordance with modern technique and considerably augmented by exercises and studies by J. Maire. Leduc 1956. 3 vols. (172, 171, 119 p.) (h.s.-c.)

Beeler, Walter. Method for the Cornet (Trumpet). Remick 1948, 1962. 2 vols. (58, 48 p.) (g.s.-h.s.)

————. Play Away! (Method). GSchirmer 1960. 32 p. (g.s.-j.h.)

Bitsch, Marcel. 20 Etudes. Leduc 1954. 20 p. (c.)

Bordogni-Porret. 24 Vocalises. Leduc 1951. 24 p. (h.s.-c.)

Bousquet, N. 36 Celebrated Studies. (E. F. Goldman) CFischer 1890. 39 p. (h.s.)

Boutry, Roger. 12 Etudes de virtuosité. Leduc 1963. 23 p. (c.)

Canty, Daniel J. Bugle Signals, Calls and Marches. Ditson (Presser) 1910. 00 p.

Charlier, Theo. 36 Etudes transcendantes. rev. ed. Leduc 1946. 72 p. (c.)

Chaynes, Charles. 15 Etudes. Leduc 1959. 15 p. (c.)

Clodomir, P. 70 Little Studies. (E. Foveau) IMC n.d. 27 p. (j.h.-h.s.)

Colin, Charles, and "Bugs" Bower. Rhythms. Colin 1950, 1958. 2 vols. (paged continuously, 24 p. ea) (j.h.-h.s.)

Dubois, Pierre Max. 12 Etudes variées. Leduc 1959. 12 p. (c.)

Dufresne, Gaston. Develop Sight Reading. (R. Voisin) Colin 1954. 59 p. (h.s.-c.)

Friese, Ernst August. Neuzeitliche Studien. HofL 1953, 1958. 2 vols. (12, 26 p.) (h.s.-c.)

Gates, Everett. Odd Meter Etudes. New York, D. Gornston, 1962. 24 p. (h.s.-c.)

Getchell, Robert W. First Book of Practical Studies. (N. W. Hovey) Belwin 1948. 32 p. (g.s.-j.h.)

————. Second Book of Practical Studies. (N. W. Hovey) Belwin 1948. 32 p. (j.h.-h.s.)

Hering, Sigmund. Trumpet Course. I: The Beginning Trumpeter. II: The Advancing Trumpeter. III: The Progressing Trumpeter. IV:

The Achieving Trumpeter. CFischer 1958-61. 4 vols. (32 p. ea)
(j.h.-h.s.)
Kinyon, John. Breeze-Easy Method for Trumpet. Witmark 1958, 1959.
2 vols. (32 p. ea) (g.s.-j.h.)
Nagel, Robert. Speed Studies. Mentor 1965. 31 p. (h.s.-c.)
Schaefer, August H. The Professional's Key to Double, Triple, Fan-Fare
(Utility) Tonguing. CFischer 1938. 35 p. (h.s.-c.)
Schantl-Pottag. Preparatory Melodies to Solo Work. Belwin 1948. 40 p.
(j.h.-h.s.)
Smith, Walter M. Lip Flexibility on the Cornet or Trumpet. CFischer
1935. 19 p. (h.s.-c.)
————. Top Tones for the Trumpeter. CFischer 1936. 67 p. (c.)
van der Woude, Mary. Advanced Virtuoso Works. Colin 1964. 2 vols.
(18 p. ea) (h.s.-c.)
————. Pre Virtuoso Studies. Colin 1963. 23 p. (j.h.-h.s.)
Voxman, Himie, comp. & ed. Selected Studies for Cornet or Trumpet.
Rubank 1953. 76 p. (h.s.)

*

Bozza, Eugène. 12 Etudes-caprices. Leduc 1944. 17 p. sax (c.)
Karg-Elert, Sigfrid. 25 Capricen und Sonate, Op. 153. Frankfurt/Main,
W. Zimmermann, 1965. 2 vols. (21, 27 p.) sax (c.)
————. Etüden-Schule, Op. 41. (W. Gerlach) HofL 1953. 32 p.
oboe (c.)

HORN METHODS AND STUDIES

Beeler, Walter. Play Away! (Method). GSchirmer 1960. 32 p. (g.s.-j.h.)
Bitsch, Marcel. 12 Etudes. Leduc 1959. 15 p. (c.)
Bozza, Eugène. 18 Etudes en forme d'improvisation. Leduc 1961. 15 p.
(c.)
Chaynes, Charles. 15 Etudes. Leduc 1959. 15 p. (c.)
Conord, Charles. 45 Etudes de déchiffrage et de transposition. Lemoine
1958. 33 p. (c.)
Devémy, Jean. 21 Lectures-études et 9 études d'examens. Paris, P.
Fougères (Leduc) 1946. 20 p. (c.)
Getchell, Robert W. First Book of Practical Studies. Belwin 1961. 32 p.
(g.s.-j.h.)
————. Second Book of Practical Studies. Belwin 1961. 32 p. (j.h.-h.s.)
Howe, Marvin. Method for the French Horn. Remick n.d. 61 p.
(g.s.-h.s.)
Kinyon, John. Breeze-Easy Method for French Horn. Witmark 1958,
1959. 2 vols. (32 p. ea) (g.s.-h.s.)
Krol, Bernhard. Waldhorn-Studien für die Unterstufe. Hamburg, D.
Rahter, 1963. 10 p. (g.s.-j.h.)
Liebert, Heinz. 25 Spezialstudien für tiefes Horn. HofL 1965. 28 p.
(c.)

Maxime-Alphonse. 200 Etudes nouvelles mélodiques et progressives.
    I.   70 Etudes très faciles et faciles. 28 p.
    II. 40 Etudes faciles. 22 p.
    III. 40 Etudes moyenne force. 24 p.
    IV. 20 Etudes difficiles. 19 p.
    V. 20 Etudes très difficiles. 23 p.
    VI. 10 Grandes études nouvelles mélodiques et de virtuosité. 27 p.
    Leduc 1920-1925. 6 vols. (h.s.-c.)
Paul, Ernst. Waldhornschule: Bd. I: Anfangsgründe. Doblinger 1948.
    40 p. (g.s.-j.h.)
—————. Bd. II: 50 neue melodische Etüden. Doblinger 1947. 43 p.
    (j.h.-c.)
—————. Bd. III: 100 technische Studien. Doblinger 1952. 2 vols.
    (paged continuously: 1-47, 48-73) (h.s.-c.)
—————. Bd. IV: 60 neue Etüden zur Erlernung des Transponierens.
    Doblinger 1947. [62 p.] (c.)
Reynolds, Verne. 48 Etudes. GSchirmer 1961. 53 p. (c.)
—————. 16 Studies . . . [after] Kreutzer. GSchirmer 1964. 24 p. (c.)
Schantl-Pottag. Preparatory Melodies to Solo Work. Belwin 1941. 40 p.
    (j.h.-h.s.)
Thévet, Lucien. 00 Etudes. Leduc 1963. 2 vols. (11 p. ea) (j.h.-h.s.)
—————. 65 Etudes-déchiffrages. Leduc 1967. 23 p. (h.s.-c.)
—————. Méthode complète. Leduc 1960. 2 vols. (paged continuously,
    338 p.) (h.s. c.)
van der Woude, Mary. Advanced Virtuoso Works. Colin 1964. 2 vols.
    (18 p. ea) (h.s.-c.)
—————. Pre Virtuoso Studies. Colin 1963. 23 p. (j.h.-h.s.)
Weber, Alain. 13 Etudes. Leduc 1959. 13 p. (h.s.-c.)

TROMBONE METHODS AND STUDIES

Beeler, Walter. Method for the Trombone. Remick 1944, 1962. 2 vols.
    (71, 48 p.) (g.s.-h.s.)
—————. Method for Baritone (Euphonium). Remick 1946, 1962. 2
    vols. (g.s.-h.s.)
—————. Play Away! (Method). GSchirmer 1960. 32 p. (g.s.-j.h.)
Bernard, Paul. Méthode complète pour trombone basse, tuba, saxhorns
    basses et contrebasses. Leduc 1960. 136 p. (c.)
Bitsch, Marcel. 15 Etudes de rhythme. Leduc 1956. 16 p. (c.)
Blazhevich, Vladislav. Clef Studies. Leeds 1948. 88 p. (h.s.-c.)
—————. Sequences for Trombone; 26 Melodic Studies in Varied
    Rhythms and Keys. CFischer, IMC, n.d. (h.s.-c.)
Blèger, M. 31 Brilliant Studies. Cundy-B n.d. 19 p. (h.s.-c.)
Blume, O. 36 Studies for Trombone with F Attachment. (R. Fink)
    CFischer 1962. 45 p. (h.s.-c.)

Bordogni-Rochut. Melodious Etudes. CFischer 1928. 3 vols. (87, 65, 79 p.) (h.s.-c.)

Boutry, Roger. 12 Etudes de haut perfectionnement. Leduc 1958. 19 p. (c.)

Cimera, Jaroslav. 221 Progressive Studies. Belwin 1942. 48 p. (g.s.-j.h.)

Colin, Charles. Progressive Technique. Colin 1958. 22 p. (j.h.-h.s.)

—————, and "Bugs" Bower. Rhythms. Colin 1950, 1958. 2 vols. (paged continuously, 24 p. ea) (j.h.-h.s.)

Dufresne, Gaston. Develop Sight Reading. (R. Voisin) Colin 1954. 31 p. (h.s.-c.)

Hering, Sigmund. 40 Progressive Etudes. CFischer 1964. 42 p. (j.h.-h.s.)

Kahila, Kauko. Advanced Studies (in Tenor and Alto Clefs). RKing n.d. 16 p. (c.)

Kinyon, John. Breeze-Easy Method for Trombone. Witmark 1958, 1959. 2 vols. (32 p. ea) (g.s.-j.h.)

Lafosse, André. Méthode complète. Leduc 1921. 2 vols. (paged continuously, 280 p.) (h.s.-c.)

Ostrander, Allen. The F Attachment and Bass Trombone. (C. Colin) New Sounds in Modern Music (Colin) 1956. 40 p. (h.s.-c.)

—————. Method for Bass Trombone and F Attachment for Tenor Trombone. CFischer 1966. 48 p. (h.s.-c.)

—————. Shifting Meter Studies for Bass Trombone or Tuba (Annotated for Bass Trombone with Double Valve). RKing 1965. 20 p. (c.)

Pichaureau, Gérard. 20 Etudes. Leduc 1963. 20 p. (c.)

VanderCook, H. A. Etudes. (W. C. Welke) Rubank 1957. 40 p. (j.h.-h.s.)

van der Woude, Mary. Pre Virtuoso Studies. Colin 1964. 23 p. (j.h.-h.s.)

Voxman, Himie, comp. & ed. Selected Studies for Trombone. Rubank 1952. 72 p. (j.h.-h.s.)

—————. Selected Studies for Baritone. Rubank 1952. 72 p. (j.h.-h.s.)

TUBA METHODS AND STUDIES

Beeler, Walter. Method for the Tuba. Remick 1946, 1962. 2 vols. (67, 48 p.) (g.s.-h.s.)

—————. Play Away! (Method). GSchirmer 1960. 32 p. (g.s.-j.h.)

Blazhevich, Vladislav. 70 Studies. GMI 1959 (O/P); RKing n.d. 103 p. (c.)

Cimera, Jaroslav. 73 Advanced Tuba Studies. Belwin 1955. 31 p. (h.s.-c.)

Getchell, Robert W. First Book of Practical Studies. (N. W. Hovey) Belwin 1955. 31 p. (g.s.-j.h.)

—————. Second Book of Practical Studies. (N. W. Hovey) Belwin 1955. 31 p. (j.h.-h.s.)

Kinyon, John. Breeze Easy Method for Tuba. Witmark 1958, 1959.
2 vols. (32 p. ea) (g.s.-j.h.)
Maenz, Otto. 12 Spezialstudien. HofL 1965. 16 p. (c.)
Ostrander, Allen. Shifting Meter Studies for Bass Trombone or Tuba.
RKing 1965. 20 p. (h.s.-c.)
Vasil'ev, S. Etudes. GMI 1960 (1-30) (O/P); RKing n.d. (1-24). (47
or 39 p.) (c.)

TRUMPET ENSEMBLES

Cassel, Don, and Livingston Gearhart. Trumpet Sessions. Shawnee 1950.
56 p. 2-4 trpts (h.s.) score only
Schneider, Willy. Erstes Trompetenspiel. SchottM 1960. 32 p. 1-3 trpts
(g.s.)

TRUMPET DUETS

Butterworth, Arthur. 3 Dialogues. Hinrichsen 1962. (h.s.-c.)
Cabus, P. Duo. Maurer 1963. (I: a'') (j.h.-h.s.)
Castérède, Jacques. 6 Pièces brèves en duo. Leduc 1965. (I: c''';
II: b'') (h.s.-c.)
de Guide, Richard. Duo. Leduc 1958. (I: c''') (c.) parts only
Ehmann, Wilhelm, comp. Geistliches Zweierspiel für Bläser. BVK
2/1956. 156 p. (g.s.-c.)
Gates, Everett. Odd Meter Duets. New York, Gate Music Co. (Gorns-
ton) 1964. 24 p. (I: a'') (h.s.-c.)
Gearhart, Livingston. Duet Sessions. Shawnee 1964. 64 p. (h.s.)
Hering, Sigmund, comp. & arr. Miniature Classics. CFischer 1960. 31 p.
(j.h.)
————. More Miniature Classics. CFischer 1962. 31 p. (j.h.-h.s.)
————. Trumpets for 2. CFischer 1966. 31 p. (j.h.-h.s.)
Lachowska, Stefania. Duety. PWM 1965. 8 p. (j.h.)
McMullen, Patrick. 3 Movements. Shawnee 1966. (I: b♭'') (h.s.-c.)
Norby, Erik. 3 Suites. Hansen 1961. (g.s.-j.h.)
————. 3 Suites II. Hansen 1962. (g.s.-j.h.)
————. 2-Stemmig Trompetmusik. Hansen 1963. (j.h.)
Rebner, Wolfgang. Inventionen. Munich, Edition Modern, 1961. (I:
d'''/e'''; II: b'') (c.)
Schäfer, Karl. Spielstücke für 2 Trompeten. BVK 1959. 21 p. (j.h.-h.s.)
Schneider, Willy, comp. & ed. Klassische Spielstücke. BVK 1956. 16 p.
(g.s.-h.s.)
Seeboth, Max. 3 Duette. Noetzel 1962. (I: b♭'') (c.)
Voxman, Himie, comp. & ed. Selected Duets. Rubank 1951. 2 vols.
(72 p. ea) (I: j.h.; II: h.s.)

Weichlein, Roman. Trompetenduette (1695). (H. Kümmerling) HofL 1953. 15 p. (I: c''') (h.s.-c.)

＊

Arma, Paul. Music on French Folk Tunes. UniversalL 1957. 2 rec (j.h.)

Badings, Henk. Kleine Suite. Amsterdam, Heuwekemeijer, 1950. 2 rec (I & II: a'') (j.h.-h.s.)

Becker, Heinz, comp. & ed. Klarinetten-Duette aus der Frühzeit des Instrumentes. BreitkopfW 1954. 13 p. (I: b''/d'''; II: b'') (c.)

Boismortier, Joseph Bodin de. Sonata, Op. 6, No. 6 (Paris 1725). (F. Raugel) BVK n.d. (HM 85) 2 fl (I & II: d''') (c.)

Chédeville, Esprit Philippe. Kleine Weihnachtsmusik. (A. von Arx) BVK [pref. 1951] 2 rec (g.s.-h.s.)

————. 6 galante Duos. (A. von Arx) BVK [pref. 1951] (HM 81) 2 rec (h.s.-c.)

Dietrich, Fritz, comp. & arr. Aus Leopold Mozarts Notenbuch. BVK n.d. 16 p. 2 rec (I: a'') (h.s.)

Doflein, Erich, comp. & arr. Der Fuchstanz und andere Volkstänze. BVK n.d. 15 p. 2 rec (g.s.-h.s.)

————. Leichte Duette. BVK 1955, 1957. 2 vols. (16 p. ea) 2 rec (g.s.-h.s.)

Dolmetsch, Carl, comp. & arr. Music from Shakespeare's Plays. UniversalL 1958. 11 p. 2 rec (I: g''/c''') (h.s.-c.)

Gastoldi, Giovanni Giacomo. Spielstücke (Milan 1598). (E. Kiwi) BVK n.d. (HM 23) 2 unspecified insts (I: c''') (c.)

Giesbert, F. J., comp. & arr. Aus dem Barock. SchottM 1938. 31 p. 2 rec (I: a''/c''') (h.s.-c.)

————. Barocke Spielstücke. SchottM n.d. 2 vols. 2 rec (I: a''/c''') (h.s.-c.)

Guillemant, Benoist. Suite (1746). (W. Gianinni) Heinrichshofen 1962. 2 rec (I: a'') (h.s.-c.)

Hoffmann, Adolf, comp. & arr. Deutsche Dorfmusik. SchottM n.d. 16 p. 2 rec (I: g''/a'') (g.s.-h.s.)

Korda, Viktor, comp. & arr. Volksmusik aus Oesterreich. SchottM n.d. 16 p. 2 rec (I: g''/a'') (g.s.-h.s.)

Lasso, Orlando di. Bicinien (Nuremberg 1610). (G. Pinthus) BVK n.d. (HM 2) 2 rec (j.h.-c.)

————. 6 Fantasien. (W. Pudelko) BVK n.d. (HM 18) 2 rec (h.s.-c.)

Lavigne, Philibert de. 2 leichte Suiten (Paris 1731). (H. Ruf) Lörrach/ Bd., Deutscher Ricordi, 1956. 2 rec (I & II: c''') (h.s.-c.)

Matthes, René, comp. & arr. Aus einem Spielbuch von 1740. BVK [pref. 1949] 15 p. 2 rec, opt perc (g.s.-j.h.)

Mönkemeyer, Helmut, comp. & arr. Meister des 16. und 17. Jahrhunderts; Spielstücke. Pelikan 1960. (Musica instrumentalis 4) 16 p. 2 unspecified insts (I: a'') (j.h.-c.)

Nowak, Leopold, comp. & ed. Bicinien der Renaissance. BVK n.d.
(HM 27) 8 p. 2 unspecified insts (j.h.-c.)
Poser, Hans. Spiel- und Tanzstücke. Sikorski 1954. 19 p. 2 rec
(I: g''/a'') (g.s.-j.h.)
Pudelko, Walther, comp. & arr. Leichte Duette alter Meister des 16.
Jahrhunderts. BVK n.d. (HM 4) 11 p. 2 rec (j.h.-c.)
Rhaw, Georg, comp. & ed. Bicinia gallica et latina (Wittenberg 1545).
(H. Mönkemeyer) Heinrichshofen 1963. vol. I 2 unspecified insts
(I: a'') (j.h.-c.)
Rotenbucher, Erasmus, comp. & ed. Schöne und liebliche Zwiegesänge
(Diphona amoena et florida) (Nuremberg 1549). (D. Degen)
BVK [pref. 1942] (HM 74) 2 unspecified insts (I: g''/a'')
(h.s.-c.)
Sweelinck, Jan Pieterszon. Rimes françoises et italiennes (Amsterdam
1612). (J. P. Hinnenthal) BVK [pref. 1951] (HM 75) (h.s.-c.)
Vierdanck, Johann. Capricci (Rostock 1641). (H. Engel) BVK n.d.
(HM 21) 2-3 cornetti (I: b♭''; II: a'') (c.) score only
Voreck, Emanuel, comp. & arr. Volkstänze aus dem Bayrischen Wald.
SchottM n.d. 2 rec (I: a'') (g.s.-h.s.)
Walter, Johann. Kanons in den Kirchentönen. (W. Ehmann) BVK
³/1954. (HM 63) 2 unspecified insts (c.)

TRUMPET TRIOS

Bach, Carl Philipp Emanuel. March (Fanfare) (Wq. 188). (E. Simon)
Marks n.d. 3 tpts, timp (I. a'') (j.h.-h.s.)
Brugk, Hans Melchior. 10 kleine Vortragsstücke. Grosch n.d. (g.s.-h.s.)
Cabus, P. 3 Mouvements. Maurer 1963. (I: a'') (h.s.-c.)
Donato, Anthony. Sonatina. GSchirmer 1954. (I: b'') (h.s.-c.)
Elwell, Herbert. Fanfares Strictly for Trumpets. Colin 1962. (I: a'')
(j.h.-h.s.)
Goldman, Richard Franko, comp. & ed. 5 Pre-Classical Pieces. New
York, Music Press, 1942. (works by Purcell, Philidor, and Anon.)
3 trpts, opt perc (I: a'') (j.h.-h.s.)
Herbert, Victor. Just for Fun. CFischer 1950. 3 cts, snare drum, bass
drum (j.h.-h.s.)
Ketting, Otto. "Kleine Suite" (1957). Donemus 1957. (h.s.-c.)
Knight, Vincent, comp. & arr. 10 Trios. London, Ascherberg, Hopwood
& Crew (GSchirmer) 1960. 19 p. (g.s.-j.h.)
Levy, Ernst. Fanfares (1947). New York, A. Broude, 1957. (I: b'';
II: g♯'') (c.)
Muczynski, Robert. Trumpet Trio, Op. 11, No. 1. GSchirmer 1961.
(I: b'') (h.s.-c.)
Nelhybel, Vaclav. Musica festiva. FColombo 1965. (j.h.-h.s.)
————. 12 Concert Pieces. FColombo 1965. (j.h.-h.s.)

Osborne, Willson. 4 Fanfares Based on 18th-century French Hunting Calls. RKing 1958. 3 trpts, timp (I & II: a'') (h.s.-c.)
Phillips, Burrill. Trio. RKing 1961. (I: b''; II: a'') (c.)
Presser, William. Suite. Tritone 1962. (I: b♭'') (j.h.-c.)
Schäfer, Karl. Spielstücke für 3 Trompeten. BVK 1959. 20 p. (j.h.-h.s.)
Stein, Leon. Trio. Merion (Presser) 1958. (I: b♭'') (h.s.-c.)
Tomasi, Henri. Suite. Leduc 1964. (I: a♯''; II: a♭''; III: a'') (h.s.-c.)

*

Mattheson, Johann. Suite in G (Op. 1, No. 5). (E. H. Hunt) SchottL 1941. 3 rec (I-III: a'') (h.s.-c.)
Mönkemeyer, Helmut, comp. & arr. Musik aus dem Frühbarock. SchottM 1958. 23 p. 3 rec (I: a'') (h.s.-c.) score only
—————. Musik aus dem Hochbarock. SchottM 1960. 23 p. 3 rec (I: a'') (h.s.-c.) score only
—————. Musik aus der Vorklassik. SchottM 1961. 23 p. 3 rec (I: a'') (h.s.-c.) score only
Vierdanck, Johann. Capricci (Rostock 1641). (H. Engel) BVK n.d. (HM 21) 2-3 cornetti (I:b♭''; II: a'') (c.) score only

TRUMPET QUARTETS, ETC.

Altenburg, Johann Ernst (attr.). Concerto for Clarini and Timpani (Halle 1795). (R. King) RKing 1956. 7 trpts, timp (I, II, V, VI: c'''; III: b♭'') (h.s.-c.)
Lo Presti, Ronald. Suite for 5 Trumpets. Shawnee 1963. (I: b''; II: a'') (h.s.-c.)
Neukomm, Sigismund. 3 Fanfares. (D. Townsend) New York, Beekman Music (Mercury) 1965. (I: c'''; II: a'') (h.s.-c.)
Reynolds, Verne. Music for 5 Trumpets. RKing 1964. (I: c♯'''; II: c'''; III: b♭''; IV: g♯''; V: a♭'') (c.)
Scheidt-King. Canzon (Hamburg 1621). RKing 1959. (I & II: a'') (h.s.-c.)
Seiff, Jakob. Bayrische Fanfaren (ca.1820). (E. F. Schmid) BVK n.d. 4 trpts, opt timp (j.h.-h.s.) parts only
Streck, Peter. Fränkische Fanfaren (ca.1840). (E. F. Schmid) BVK n.d. 4 trpts, opt timp (j.h.-h.s.) parts only
Zelenka, Johann Dismas. 6 Reiterfanfaren. (K. Janetzky) HofL 1962. 4 trpts, timp (I: c'''; II: a'') (h.s.-c.)

HORN DUETS

Anon. 24 Englische Duette [24 Select Duets] (London n.d.). (H. Erdmann) BVK 1965. (Kleine Blasmusikhefte) (I: f''/b♭'') (h.s.-c.)

Bates, William. Flourishes for Brass [Duettinos] (London 1770?). (C. Curwin) Chappell 1965. 2 trpts/hns (h.s.-c.)

Duvernoy, Frédéric. 20 Horn Duets. (E. A. Wienandt) SouthernSA 1967. (I: g''/c''') (h.s.-c.)

Ehmann, Wilhelm, comp. Geistliches Zweierspiel für Bläser. BVK 2/1956. 156 p. (g.s.-c.)

Gipps, Ruth. A Taradiddle, Opuscule 51. Williams 1961. (I: a♮'') (h.s.-c.)

[Hoss, Wendell, comp. & ed.] 60 Selected Duets; Duets by Los Angeles Horn Club. SouthernSA 1966. 48 p. (j.h.-c.)

Kopprasch, Wilhelm. 8 Duets. (R. François) IMC 1958. (I: c''') (h.s.-c.) parts only

Korda, Viktor. 5 Bagatellen. Doblinger 1966. (I: g''/a♭'') (h.s.-c.)

Mayer, Rudolph. 12 Bicinia. Shawnee 1965. (I: g''/a♭'') (h.s.-c.)

Métral, Pierre. Pièces en duo. Paterson 1963. (I: c''') (h.s.-c.)

Mozart, Wolfgang Amadeus. 12 Duets, K. 487. (J. Marx) McG&M 1055; (O. Stösser) HofF 1061. (I: c''') (c.)

Nicolai, Otto. Duet No. 1. (K. Janetzky) MRara 1961. (I: b'') (h.s.-c.)

————. Duet No. II. MRara 1965. (I: b♭'') (h.s.-c.)

————. 3 Duette [i.e. Duet No. III?] (O. Stösser) HofH n.d. (I: b'') (h.s.-c.)

————. Duets Nos. 4, 5, & 6. (M. Buyanovsky) MRara 1966. (I: a''/c''') (h.s.-c.)

Rimsky-Korsakov, Nikolay Andreyevitch. 2 Duets. (R. King) RKing 1959. (j.h.-h.s.)

Rossini, Gioacchino. 5 Duos. (E. Leloir) Simrock 1961. (j.h.-h.s.)

Schenk-Reynolds. 6 Sonatas, Op. 8. N. Y., MCA Music, 1967. (I & II: a'') (c.)

Schuller, Gunther. Duets. Oxford 1962. (I: b''; II: b♭'') (c.)

Stösser, Otto, comp. & ed. Duette alter Meister. HofF n.d. 2 vols. (15, 16 p.) (I: g''/c''') (j.h.-h.s.)

Twinn, Sydney, comp. & arr. 12 Old English Songs. London, Augener (Galaxy) 1959. (j.h.-h.s.)

Voxman, Himie, comp. & ed. Selected Duets. Rubank 1958. 2 vols. (72 p. ea) (hn I: g'/c''') (I: j.h.; II: h.s.)

*

Degen, Dietz, comp. & ed. Fröhliche Jagd. BVK [pref. 1939]. 1-2 rec (j.h.-h.s.)

Kleines Haydn-Heft. BVK 1960. 2 rec (I: d''/b♭'') (h.s.-c.)

Telemann, Georg Philipp. Kleine Stücke. (A. Hoffmann) BVK [pref. 1935]. (I: f''/b♭'') (h.s.-c.)

HORN TRIOS

Cowell, Henry. Hymn and Fuguing Tune No. 12. AMP 1960. (I, II: a''; III: a♭'') (h.s.-c.)

Duvernoy, Frédéric. 4 Trios. (M. Zimolong) Sikorski 1963. parts only (E. A. Wienandt) SouthernSA 1967. score and parts (I: c''') (h.s.-c.)

Reicha, Anton. 6 Trios, Op. 82. (A. Frehse-F. von Glasenapp-J. Chambers) IMC 1958. (I: a'') (h.s.-c.)

————. 8 Trios, Op. 82. (E. Leloir) Simrock 1964. (I: e''/c'''; II: a'/a'') (h.s.-c.)

HORN QUARTETS, ETC.

Arnell, Richard. Music for Horns, Op. 82. SouthernNY 1965. (I: b♭'') (h.s.-c.)

Bozza, Eugène. Suite. Leduc 1952. (I: b♭'') (h.s.-c.)

Cadow, Paul. 3 Stücke. Osthofen (Rhh.), Verlag "Das Bläserschiff," n.d. (j.h.)

Castelnuovo-Tedesco, Mario. Chorale with Variations, Op. 162. Elkan 1956. (I: b'') (h.s.-c.)

Clark, Frank. St. Hubert's Hunting Song. EMusicus 1960. (j.h.)

Flothuis, Marius. 4 Invenzioni, Op. 64 (1963). Donemus 1964. (I: c''') (h.s.-c.)

Gallay, Jacques François. Grand Quartet, Op. 26. (E. Leloir) Amsterdam, Edition KaWe, 1967. (h.s.-c.) parts only

Harris, Albert. Theme and Variations for 8 Horns. RKing 1960. (I: c'''; II: b''; III-V: a'') (h.s.-c.)

Harris, Arthur. Theme and Variations. Shawnee 1963. (h.s.-c.)

Hindemith, Paul. Sonate (1952). SchottM 1953. (I: a'') (c.)

Janetzky, Kurt, comp. & ed. Jägerstücklein. HofL 1955. 14 p. 3-4 hns (j.h.-h.s.)

Kay, Ulysses. Serenade No. 2. n.p., Duchess Music Corp. (Leeds) 1964. (I: a''/b''; III: a♭'') (h.s.-c.)

Lo Presti, Ronald. Second Suite. Shawnee 1962. (I: a'') (h.s.-c.)

Lütgen, W. A. Quartett, Op. 19. (K. Janetzky) HofL 1953. (I: c'''; III: a'') (h.s.-c.)

Mayer, Rudolph. 4 Little Pieces. SouthernSA 1963. (h.s.)

Palestrina-Schultz. Christe, lux vera. Kendor 1962. (j.h.-h.s.)

Rein, Walter. Divertimento. SchottM 1961. (h.s.)

————. Waldmusik. SchottM 1961. (h.s.)

Reynolds, Verne. Short Suite. RKing 1960. (I: b'') (c.)

Rimsky-Korsakov, Nikolay Andreyevitch. Notturno. (R. King) RKing 1957. (j.h.-h.s.)

Rossini, Gioacchino. Le Rendez-vous de chasse. McG&M 1962. parts only) (E. Leloir) Simrock 1963. score and parts (h.s.)

Schuller, Gunther. 5 Pieces for 5 Horns (1952). Florence, A. Bruzzi-
    chelli, 1965. (I: c♯''' ; II: a'' ; III: c''' ; IV & V: a♭'') (c.)
Tcherepnin, Nicolas. 6 Quartette. Bad Godesberg, R. Forberg, 1956.
    (I: a'') (h.s.-c.)
Tippett, Michael. Sonata. SchottL 1957. (I & III: c''' ; II: a'') (c.)
Vittoria-Schultz. O sacrum convivium. Kendor 1962. (j.h.-h.s.)
Weber, Friedrich Dionys. 3 Quartette. (K. Janetzky) HofL 1953.
    (I & II: c''') (h.s.-c.)

TROMBONE ENSEMBLES

Gearhart, L., D. Cassel, and W. Hornibrook. Bass Clef Sessions. Shawnee
    1954. 55 p. 2-4 trbs (h.s.)

TROMBONE DUETS

Blazhevich, Vladislav. Concert Duets. Leeds 1947. 62 p. (I: a♭'/c♯'' ;
    II: f'/a') (h.s.-c.)
Cornette, Victor. 6 Concert Duets. Cundy-B n.d. (I & II: f'/c'')
    (h.s.-c.)
Ehmann, Wilhelm, comp. Geistliches Zweierspiel für Bläser. BVK
    2/1956. 156 p. (g.s.-c.)
Russo, William. Duets, Op. 35. New York, M. Brown (Colin) 1961.
    16 p. (I: d'/b♭') (h.s.)
Voxman, Himie, comp. & ed. Selected Duets. Rubank 1958. 2 vols.
    (72 p. ea) (I: e♭'/b♭') (I: j.h.; II: h.s.)

❋

Devienne, François. Duos concertants, Op. 3. (E. Hess) Basel, Edition
    Kneusslin, 1960. 2 bn (I & II: g'/a') (c.) parts only
Edelstein, Heinz, comp. & ed. Rokoko-Duette. Moeck 1956. (Moecks
    Kammermusik 39, 45) 2 vols. 2 vc (I: g'; II: f'/g') (c.) (I:
    J. B. de Boismortier. Sonatas, Op. 14, No. 3; Op. 40, No. 3; II:
    Boismortier. Sonatas, Op. 40, Nos. 1-2. — M. Corrette. Sonata,
    Op. 24)
de Fesch, Willem. 6 Sonate, Op. 8, Nos. 7-12 (London ca.1736-8). (L.
    Schäffler) Moeck 1940. (Moecks Kammermusik 19, 20) 2 vols.
    2 vc (I: a') (h.s.-c.)
Gebauer, François René. 3 Duos concertants, Op. 8. (J. Thonton)
    SouthernSA 1965. 2 bn (I: d''/e♭'' ; II: a♭'/b♭') (c.)
Lasso, Orlando di. 6 Fantasien. (W. Pudelko) BVK n.d. (HM 18)
    2 rec (c.)
Nowak, Leopold, comp. & ed. Bicinien der Renaissance. BVK n.d.
    (HM 27) 8 p. 2 unspecified insts (j.h.-c.)

Ozi, Etienne. 3 Kleine Sonaten [Sonates faciles] (Leipzig n.d.) (F. von Glasenapp-A. Karl) HofL 1953. 2 bn (I: g'; II: f'/g') (h.s.-c.)

Pudelko, Walther, comp. & arr. Leichte Duette alter Meister des 16. Jahrhunderts. BVK n.d. (HM 4) 11 p. 2 rec (j.h.-c.)

Rhaw, Georg, comp. & ed. Bicinia gallica et latina (Wittenberg 1545). (H. Mönkemeyer) Heinrichshofen 1963. vols. I & II 2 unspecified insts (I: f''/a'' – treble clef) (h.s.-c.)

Schneider, Georg Abraham. Duette. (O. Pischkitl – K. U. Kraehnke) HofL 1956. 2 bn, etc. (I: g'/c''; II: f'/b♭') (h.s.-c.)

Walter, Johann. Kanons in den Kirchentönen. (W. Ehmann) BVK ³/1954. (HM 63) 2 unspecified insts (c.)

TROMBONE TRIOS

Bruckner, Anton. Aequale. Ensemble 1965. (I: b♭') (h.s.-c.)

Lotti-Dedrick. Vere languores nostros. Kendor 1963. (h.s.)

Moulaert, Raymond. Suite (1939). CeBeDeM 1959. (I & II: a'; III: g') (h.s.-c.)

Premru, Raymond. 2 Pieces. Ensemble 1965. (I: b♭') (h.s.-c.)

Schumann-Fote. Fugue, Op. 68. Kendor 1966. (I: b♭'/d''; III: g♭') (h.s.-c.)

Speer, Daniel. 2 Sonatas (Ulm 1687). (A. Baines) MRara 1961. (I: b'; II: f♯') (h.s.-c.)

Tanner, Paul. Imitation. Holly-Pix 1966. (I: a♭') (h.s.)

*

Kummer, Gotthilf Heinrich. Trios, Op. 11, Op. 13. (F. von Glasenapp – A. Karl) HofL 1953. 3 bn (I: f'/a') (h.s.-c.)

TROMBONE QUARTETS, ETC.

Ameller, André. Chorale. Hinrichsen 1960. (I: b♭'; II: g♭') (h.s.-c.)

Bach-King. 16 Chorales. RKing 1958. 16 p. (I: f'/a') (h.s.-c.)

Bassett, Leslie. Quartet. RKing 1954. (I: b'; II & III: b♭'; IV: g') (c.)

Beethoven, Ludwig van. 3 Equali. Breitkopf n.d. (I: c''; II: a♭') parts only (R. King) RKing 1961. (I: b♭'; II: g♭') (h.s.-c.) score and parts

Beethoven-Dedrick. Miserere – Amplius. Kendor 1964. (I: f'/g') (j.h.-h.s.)

Boutry, Roger. 5 Pièces a quatre. Leduc 1961. (I: f''; II: d''; III: b'; IV: g♯') (c.)

Chapman, Roger. Suite of Three Cities. PetersNY 1960. (I: c'') (c.)

Charpentier, Jacques. Quatuor de forme liturgique. Leduc 1960. (I: c♯''; II: b'; III: g♯') (c.)

Defay, Jean-Michel. 4 Pièces. Leduc 1954. (I: d♯''; II & III: c♯'';
IV: a') (c.)

Dubois, Pierre Max. Quatuor. Leduc 1962. (I: c♯''; II: a') (c.)

Gabrieli, Andrea. Ricercare del 12⁰ tono. (J. K. Friedman) Ensemble
1967. (I: b') (c.)

Gabrieli, Giovanni. Sonata. (K. Brown) IMC 1966. (I & II: a♭') (c.)

Gow, David. Suite. MRara 1967. (I: d♭''; II: a'; III: f♯') (c.)

King, Robert, comp. & arr. 24 Early German Chorales. RKing 1956.
24 p. (j.h.-c.)

Langley, James. Suite. Hinrichsen 1961. (I: b♭'; II: g') (h.s.-c.)

Laudenslager, Harold. 3 Preludes and Fugues. Camara 1960. (I:
a♯'/b♯'; II: g♯'/b♭'; III: e♭'/g♯') (c.)

McCarty, Patrick. Recitative and Fugue. RKing 1960. (I: a♯'; II: a♭')
(h.s.-c.)

Marini, Biagio. Canzona, Op. 8, No. 3 (1626). (G. Smith) Ensemble
1965. (I: g') (c.)

Massaino, Tiburtio. Canzon per 8 tromboni (Venice 1608). (R. King)
RKing 1964; (C. Silliman) Ensemble 1964. (I: g') (c.)

Mendelssohn-Smith. 2 Pieces. Pro Art 1966. (I: g') (c.)

Meulemans, Arthur. Suite (1942). CeBeDeM 1958. (I: c''; II: a')
(c.)

Morley-Myers. My Bonnie Lass. Ensemble 1965. (I & II: g') (h.s.-c.)

––––––. Now is the Month of Maying. Ensemble 1965. (I: g'; II:
f♯') (h.s.-c.)

Nelhybel, Vaclav. 3 Organa. FColombo 1965. (I: b♭') (h.s.)

––––––. 6 Pieces. General 1966. (I: b♭'; II: f♯'; III: a') (h.s.)

Olander, Eino. First Suite. (H. Ferguson) GSchirmer 1951. (g.s.-j.h.)

Otten, Ludwig. Suite (1951). Donemus 1957. (I: c♯''; II: c'';
III: a') (c.)

Peeters, Flor. Suite, Op. 82. Peters 1959. (I: b'; II: g') (h.s.-c.)

Phillips, Burrill. Piece for 6 Trombones. RKing c.1953. (I: b♭'; II:
g♯'; IV: a') (c.)

Praetorius-Myers. 2 Ancient Carols (Lo, How a Rose e'er Blooming;
In dulci jubilo). Ensemble 1965. (I: g'; II: f♯') (h.s.-c.)

Purcell-Tanner. Dido's Lament from Dido and Aeneas. Holly-Pix 1965.
6 trbs (I: c♯''; II: g♯') (c.)

Rueff, Jeanine. 2 Pièces brèves. Leduc 1956. (I: b♭'; II: g') (c.)

Sanders, Robert. Scherzo and Dirge. AMP 1948. (I: b♭'; II & III:
a♭') (h.s.-c.)

Serocki, Kazimierz. Suita (1953). PWM 1954. (I: c''; II: g') (c.)

Stoltzer, Thomas. Fantasia (Hypodorian). (R. King) RKing n.d. 4 trbs,
tba [bass trb] (I & II: a') (h.s.-c.)

Telemann-Lumsden. Concerto a 4. MRara 1966. (I & II: b♭'; III: g')
(c.)

Tomasi, Henri. Etre ou ne pas être; Monologue d'Hamlet. Leduc 1963.
(I: c''; II: a♭') (c.)

TUBA DUETS

Butterfield, Don. 7 Duets. Wyckoff, N. J., DB Pub. Co., 1960. (I: b♭/c′; II: f/a) (h.s.-c.)
Goldman, Richard Franko. Duo (1948). Mercury 1950. (I: c′; II: b) (c.)

MIXED DUOS

Bach-Dedrick. Two Part Invention (No. 14). Kendor 1964. 1010 (trpt: a′′; trb: opt b♭′) (h.s.-c.)
Borden, David. 15 Dialogues. Ensemble 1962. 23 p. 1010 (trpt: g′′/d′′′; trb: f′/b′′) (c.)
Defossez, René. 4 petites pièces (1956). CeBeDeM 1957. 1(C)010 (trpt: c′′′; trb: d♯′′) (c.)
Dijk, Jan van. Sérénade (1955). Donemus 1956. 1100 (trpt: b♭′′; hn: a′′) (h.s.-c.)
Ehmann, Wilhelm, comp. Geistliches Zweierspiel. BVK ²/1956. 156 p. 1(C)010 (g.s.-c.)
Glinka-King. 4 Short Fugues. RKing 1963. 1010/1100 (g.s.-h.s.)
Kazdin, Andrew. 12 Duets. RKing 1964. 1100 (trpt: g′′/c′′′; hn: g′′/b♭′′) (h.s.-c.)
King, Robert. French Suite. RKing n.d. ct, bar (ct: c′′′; bar: g′) (j.h.-h.s.)
Kupferman, Meyer. Available Forms (1966). General 1966. 1010 (trpt: c′′′; trb: a♯′′) (c.)
Schwartz, Elliott. Essays (1966). New York, A. Broude, 1968. 1010 (trpt: c′′′, more or less; trb: g′) (c.)

✳

Hook, James. Leichte Handstücke. (W. Bergmann) SchottM 1960. 15 p. 2 rec (j.h.-h.s.)
Lasso, Orlando di. Bicinien (Nuremberg 1610). (G. Pinthus) BVK n.d. (HM 2) 2 rec (h.s.-c.)
Rhaw, Georg, comp. & ed. Bicinia gallica et latina (Wittenberg 1545). (H. Mönkemeyer) Heinrichshofen 1963. Vol. III 16 p. (h.s.-c.)

MIXED TRIOS

Ardévol, José. III Sonata a tres. Montevideo, Editorial Cooperativa Interamericana de Compositores (SouthernNY), 1945. 2(C)010 (trpt I: b′′: trb: a′) (c.)
Bachmann, Fritz, comp. Lass dir unser Lob gefallen. Rufer 1950. 144 p. 3-part settings: 1(C)020/2(C)010 (j.h.-c.) score only
Beethoven-King. Trio, Op. 87. RKing 1963. 1110/2010/1200 (trpt: a′′; hn: a′′; trb: b♭′) (h.s.-c.)

Bentzon, Niels Viggo. Trio, Op. 82 (1952). Hansen 1964. 1(C)110
(trpt: c′′′; hn: b′′; trb: c′′) (c.)

Cabus, P. Sonata a tre. Maurer 1962. 1(C)110 (trpt: a′′; hn: a′′;
trb: b′) (h.s.-c.)

Ehmann, Wilhelm, comp. Evangelisches Kantoreibuch. Rufer 3/1957.
180 p. 3-part settings: 2(C)010 (h.s.-c.) score only

Flothuis, Marius. Sonatine, Op. 26 (1945). Donemus 1946. 1(C)110
(trpt: b♭′′; hn: a′′) (h.s.-c.)

Glasser, Stanley. Trio (1958). MusicaR 1959. 2(C)010 (trpt I: b♭′′;
trb: g′) (c.)

Hughes, Mark. Divertimento. Tritone 1964. 1(C/B♭)110 (trpt in C:
c♯′′′; hn: b′′; trb: g♯′) (c.)

Josquin-de Jong. 3 Josquin Pieces. Ensemble 1966. 1110 (trpt:
g′′/b♭′′; hn: g′/a♭′) (h.s.-c.)

Knight, Morris. Cassation. Tritone 1962. 1110 (trpt: a♯′′; hn: g♯′′;
trb: b♭′) (h.s.-c.)

Kroeger, Karl. Sonata breve (1957). Tritone 1962. 1(C)110 (trpt:
b♭′′; hn: a′′; trb: b♭′) (c.)

Leclercq, Edgard. Suite classique ou suite concertante. Brogneaux
1959. 1(C)110 (trpt: b♭′′/c′′′; hn: a′′; trb: a′) (h.s.-c.)

Louël, Jean. Trio (1951). CeBeDeM 1956. 1(C)110 (trpt: b♭′′;
hn: a′′; trb: a♯′) (c.)

Marek, Robert. Trio. RKing 1959. 1110 (trpt: c♯′′′; hn: a′′; trb:
b′) (h.s.-c.)

Mayer, William. Country Fair. Boosey 1963. 2010 (trpt I: a′′;
trb: a′) (h.s.-c.)

Meulemans, Arthur. Trio (1933). Brogneaux 1950. 1(C)110 (trpt:
a′′; trb: g♯′) (h.s.-c.)

————. 2e Trio (1960). CeBeDeM 1961. 1(C)110 (trpt: b♭′′;
hn: a′′; trb: a′) (h.s.-c.)

Mozart-King. Divertimento No. 1, K.E. 439b. RKing 2/1957. 2100/
201(bar)0 (trpt 1: c′′′) (h.s.-c.)

Poulenc, Francis. Sonata (1922). London, J. & W. Chester, 1924.
1(C)110 (trpt: a′′; hn: a′′; trb: b♭′) (h.s.-c.)

Quinet, Marcel. Sonate a trois (1961). CeBeDeM 1961. 1(C)110
(trpt: b♭′′; hn: b′′; trb: g′) (c.)

Sanders, Robert. Trio. RKing 1961. 1110 (trpt: c′′′; trb: a′)
(h.s.-c.)

Scharrès, Charles. Divertimento. Brogneaux 1958. 1(C)110 (trpt:
a′′; trb: g♭′) (h.s.-c.)

Srámek, Vladimír. Trio. Prague, Státní hudební vydavatelství (Artia)
1962. 2(C)010 (trpt I: b♭′′; trb: b♭′) (c.)

✻

Davenport, LaNoue, comp. & arr. 6 American Folk Songs. Clarke & Way
1951. 3 rec [2010] (g.s.-h.s.) score only

––––––. 5 Carnival Songs of the 16th Century [Joan Domenico del Giovane da Nola]. AMP 1956. 3 rec [2010] (h.s.-c.) score only

Hook-Colwell. Terzetto. SchottL 1949. 3 rec [2010] (h.s.-c.) score only

––––––. Second Terzetto. SchottL 1961. 3 rec [2010] (h.s.-c.) score only

Hunt, Edgar H., comp. & arr. Old English Pieces for Three Recorders. SchottL 1937. [2010] (h.s.-c.) (pieces by Gibbons, Morley, Youll, Weelkes, and Robert Johnson) score only

Jaeger, Winifred, comp. & arr. 5 Canzonettas. AMP 1956. 3 rec [2010] (h.s.-c) (pieces by Marenzio, Gastoldi, and Haussmann) score only

Katz, Erich, comp. & arr. Music of the Baroque for Three Recorders. Marks 1965. 24 p. [2010] (g.s.-h.s.) (pieces by Buxtehude, Corelli, M. Franck, le Begue, et al) score only

––––––. Suite of Jewish Folk Tunes (Chanukah Melodies). New York, Omega Music Edn., 1955. 3 rec [2010] (g.s.-h.s.) score only

Mönkemeyer, Helmut, comp. & ed. Instrumentale Liedsätze um 1500. Pelikan 1960. 16 p. 3 rec [2010] (h.s.-c.) (pieces by Isaac, Hofhaimer, Clemens non Papa, et al) score only

Regnart, Jacob. 6 Lively Airs. (A. Mann) Clarke & Way c.1940. 3 rec [2010] (g.s.-c.) score only

Rossi, Salomone. 15 Canzonets (Venice 1589). (J. Newman) New York, Omega Music Corp., 1957. 3 rec [2010] (g.s.-c.) score only

––––––. 5 Sinfonie a tre voci. (E. Katz) Clarke & Way 1950. 3 rec [2010] (h.s.-c.) score only

Runge, Johannes, comp. & arr. Barocke Musizierstücke. SchottM 1962. 30 p. 3 rec [2010] (trb: f′/b♭′) (h.s.-c.) score only

Schein, Johann Hermann. 3 Canzonettas. (W. Jaeger) AMP 1954. 3 rec [2010] (trb: f′/b♭′) (h.s.-c.) score only

MIXED QUARTETS

Addison, John. Divertimento, Op. 9. Williams 1954. 2110 (trpt I: c′′′; trpt II: a♭′′; trb: g′) (h.s.-c.)

Andriessen, Jurriaan. Introduzione e allegro. Donemus 1958. 2(C)110 (trpt I: a′′; trb: g′) (h.s.-c.)

––––––. 4 Madrigali. Donemus 1962. 2(C)110 (trpt I: a′′) (j.h.-h.s.)

Bach-King. 22 Chorales. RKing 1955. 2110/2020/1210-opt tba (h.s.-c.)

––––––. March, Chorale and Fugue. RKing 1958. 2110/2020/1210-opt tba (j.h.-h.s.)

Bachmann, Fritz, comp. Lass dir unser Lob gefallen. Rufer 1950. 144 p. 4-part settings: 2(C)020 (j.h.-c.) score only

—————. Posaunenchoralbuch zum Evangelischen Kirchengesangbuch. Rufer, Merseburger 1953. unpaged 2(C)020 (j.h.-c.) score only

Bartók-Stratton. Bartók "For Children"; 5 Pieces for Brass Quartet. Boosey 1963. 2110 (g.s.-j.h.)

Bentley, Arnold, comp. & arr. XVIth Century Quartets. Chappell 1965. 2110 (g.s.-c.) (pieces by Palestrina, Vittoria, Byrd)

Berger, Jean. Intrada. RKing 1961. 2020/2110 (trpt I: b''; trb I: a♭') (h.s.-c.)

Bergsma, William. Suite. CFischer 1946. 202(trb, bar)0 (trpt I & II: c'''; bar: a♭') (c.)

Bernstein, Leonard. Fanfare for Bima. GSchirmer 1950. 1111 (trpt: c'''; hn: b''; trb: b♭'; tba: g) (c.)

Boda, John. Prelude/Scherzo/Postlude. Louisville 1965. 2110 (trpt I: b''; trb: g') (c.)

Bright, Houston. Legend & Canon. AMP 1953. 2110/2020 (trpt I: a''; trb I: b♭') (h.s.-c.)

Butterworth, Neil, comp. & arr. 4 Motets for Brass. Chappell 1967. 2110 (trpt I: a'') (h.s.-c.) (pieces by A. Gabrieli, G. Corsi, G. Aichinger, Vittoria)

—————. Tudor Suite. Chappell 1961. 2110 (h.s.) (pieces by O. Gibbons; Palestrina; T. Morley; J. Mundy, attr.)

Campra-King. Rigaudon. RKing 1960. 2020/2110-opt tba (trpt I: a''; trb I: g') (j.h.-h.s.)

Couperin-King. 2 Pieces. RKing 1959. 2110/2020-opt tba (sub trb: g') (h.s.)

Ehmann, Wilhelm, comp. & ed. Alte Spielmusik für Bläser. BVK 1964. 88 p. 4-part settings: 2(C)020 (c.) (4-part works by V. Haussmann, M. Franck, M. Praetorius, J. Staden, G. Vintz, I. Posch, P. Peuerl) score only

—————. Bläser-Intraden zum Wochenlied. BVK 1957. 127 p. 4-part settings: 2(C)020/3(C)010/1(C)030 (h.s.-c.) score only

Frackenpohl, Arthur. Quartet. RKing 1950. 2020 (trpt I: b♭''; trb I: a♭') (h.s.-c.)

Franke, Christoph, comp. Altdeutsche Volkslieder. Merseburger 1957. unpaged mostly 2020 (g.s.-j.h.) score only

Frescobaldi-Aaron. Gagliarda. CSchirmer 1953. 2020/2110 (trpt I: a'') (g.s.-j.h.)

Gabrieli, Andrea. Ricercar del duodecimo tuono. (A. Lumsden) MRara RKing n.d., 1957. separate publications 2020/2110 (trpt I: a'';

Gabrieli, Giovanni. 4 Canzoni per sonare (Venice 1608). (R. King) RKing n.d., 1967. separate publications 2020/2110 (trpt I: a''; trb I: f'/g') (A. Lumsden) MRara 1966. 2 vols. 2020/2110 (trpt I: a''; trb I: g'/b♭') (j.h.-c.)

Gardner, John. Theme and Variations, Op. 7 (1951). Oxford 1953. 2110 (trpts I & II, hn: a''; trb: a♯') (c.)

Glazunov, Alexander. In modo religioso. (R. King) RKing n.d. 1120/
2020/1210/2110-opt tba (j.h.-h.s.)

Haines, Edmund. Toccata. RKing 1949. 2020/2110 (trpt I: c′′′;
trpt II: a′′; trb I: g′) (h.s.-c.)

Handel-King. Bourrée and Minuet from The Fireworks Music. RKing
1955. 2020/2110-opt tba (trpt I: a′′; trb I: g′) (j.h.-h.s.)

Hering, Sigmund, comp. & arr. Early Classics for Brass Ensembles.
CFischer 1964. 2110 (g.s.-j.h.) (pieces by M. P. de Montéclair,
H. L. Hassler, M. Praetorius, M. Luther, and Anon.)

Hindemith, Paul. Morgenmusik. SchottM 1932. 2(C)020 (trb I: g′)
(h.s.-c.)

Hovhaness, Alan. Sharagan and Fugue. RKing 1950. 211(bar)0/
2020/3010-opt tba (trpt I: a′′; bar: a′) (j.h.-c.)

Jacob, Gordon. Scherzo. Williams 1954. 2110 (trpt I: b′′) (h.s.-c.)

Kay, Ulysses. Brass Quartet. Peer 1958. 2020 (trpt I: a′′; trb I:
g♭′) (c.)

Keller, Homer. Quartet. RKing 1954. 2110 (trpt I & II: c♯′′′; hn:
g♯′′; trb: c′′) (c.)

King, Robert, comp. & ed. 3 New England Hymns. RKing n.d. 2020/
2110/1210-opt tba (j.h.-c.)

————. Reformation Chorales. RKing 1955. 24 p. 2020/2110/1210-
opt tba (j.h.-c.)

Knight, Morris. 6 Brass Quartets. Tenuto 1966. 2020 (trpt I: b′′/
c♯′′′; trpt II: g′′/d′′′; trb I: g′/b′; trb II: f′/a′) (h.s.-c.)

Knox, Charles. Solo for Trumpet with Brass Trio. Louisville 1966.
2110/2020/1210 (trpt I: a′′) (j.h.-h.s.)

Lappi, Pietro. Canzoni 11 & 12 (Venice 1608). (A. Lumsden) MRara
1967. 2020/2110 (trpt I: a′′; trb I: a♭′/a′) (j.h.-c.)

Lasso-Butterworth. 4 Tudor Canzonas. Chappell 1961. 2110 (trpt I:
a′′) (j.h.-c.)

Lo Presti, Ronald. Miniature. Shawnee 1964. 2110 (trpt I: a′′; trb:
a′) (h.s.-c.)

Mitchell, Lyndol. Folk Suite. Rochester 1955. 2110 (trpt I: a′′/
c′′′) (h.s.-c.)

Obrecht-King. Tsat een meskin (Venice 1501). RKing 1958. 1030/
1120/1210 (trb I: a′) (h.s.-c.)

Palestrina-King. 3 Hymns. RKing 1960. 2020/2110/1210-opt tba
(trb I: g′) (g.s.-h.s.)

Phillips, Burrill. Prelude. Elkan-V 1953. 2020/2110 (trpt I: a′′)
(h.s.-c.)

Piket, Frederick. Dance & March. AMP 1952. 2020 (trpt I: b′′;
trpt II: a′′; trb I: b′; trb II: b♭′) (h.s.-c.)

Presser, William. 5 Southern Songs. Elkan 1967. 1120/2020 (trpt I:
a′′; trb I: g′) (h.s.-c.)

Purcell-Corley. 2 Trumpet Tunes and Ayre. RKing n.d. 2020/2110-
opt tba (trpt I: b′′) (j.h.-h.s.)

Purcell-King. Allegro and Air from King Arthur. RKing 1960. 2020/ 2110-opt tba (j.h.-h.s.)

————. Music for Queen Mary II. RKing 1956. 1120/2020/1210- opt tba (g.s.-c.)

Ramsöe, Wilhelm. Quartet No. 5. (R. King) RKing 1957. 211(bar) 0/202(trb, bar)0 (trpt I: c′′′; trb: c′′) (h.s.-c.)

Rasmussen, M., comp. & ed. Christmas Music. RKing 1959. 2020/ 2110-opt tba (j.h.-c.)

Raymond, Lewis. Short Suite. Avant 1964. 2110 (trpt I: b′′; trpt II: a′′; trb: a′) (h.s.-c.)

Reiche, Gottfried. 24 Neue Quatricinia (Leipzig 1696). (G. Müller) Merseburger 1958. score only (D. Miller) Ensemble 1962. score and parts Single sonatas: (D. Miller) Ensemble (1-24); (R. King) RKing (15, 18, 19, 21 & 22, 24); (A. Fromme) S. Fox (11, 12). 1030/2020/1120 (usually trpt I: a′′) (j.h.-c.)

Sanders, Robert. Suite. RKing 1956. 2020 (trpt I: b′′; trb I: f♯′) (h.s.-c.)

Schlemm, Hans Martin, comp. & ed. Lass dir unser Lob gefallen II. Merseburger 1962. 351 p. 4-part settings. 2(C)020 (j.h.-c.) score only

Schneider, Willy. Turmmusik. Noetzel 1958. 2020/2110 (j.h.-h.s.)

Schuller, Gunther. Little Brass Music (1963). Mentor 1967. 1(C)111 (trpt: d′′′; hn: b′′; trb: d′′; tba: c♯′) (c.)

Siebert, Edrich. Bees-a-buzzin'. (R. King) RKing 1958. 202(trb, bar)0 (trpt I: b♭′′; bar: a♭′) (h.s.) Also pub London, Paxton, 1954. 2 cts, E♭ alto hn, bar

Starer, Robert. Dirge. Presser 1957. 2020 (trpt I: b♭′′; trb I: g′) (h.s.-c.)

Störl, Johann Georg Christian. 6 Sonatas. (D. Miller) Ensemble 1962. 1(C)030 (trpt: a′′/b′′; trb I: g′/c′′) (c.) Sonata No. 1. (R. King) RKing 1957. 1120/2020/1030/1210-opt tba (trpt: a♭′′; sub trb: a′) (j.h.-c.)

Straesser, Joep. "Music for Brass" (1965). Donemus 1965. 2(C)110 (trpt II: b′′; hn: a′′) (c.)

Susato, Tilman, attr. 3 Dances (Antwerp 1551). (R. King) RKing 1955. 1120/2020/2110/1210-opt tba (g.s.-j.h.)

Tomkins-Butterworth. Mr. Curch's Toye and Other Pieces. Chappell 1964. 2110 (trpt I: a′′) (h.s.-c.)

White, Donald H. Serenade No. 3. Templeton 1965. 2110 (trpt I: c′′′; trpt II: b♭′′; hn: a′′; trb: d′′/d♭′′) (c.)

Wohlfahrt, Frank. Fanfaren-Musik (1958). Sikorski n.d. 2020 (trpts I & II: c′′′; trb I: c♭′′) (c.)

MIXED QUINTETS

Adler, Samuel. 5 Movements. RKing 1965. 2111 (trpt I: b′′; trpt II: a′′; hn: a♯′′; trb: a′; tba: e♭′) (c.)

Adson, John. 2 Ayres for Cornetts and Sagbuts. (R. King) RKing n.d.
    2120/2030-opt tba   (j.h.-c.)
Anon. Sonata from Die Bänkelsängerlieder. (R. King) RKing 1958.
    2120/2030/2111/2210 etc. (trpt I: a''; sub trb: g') (h.s.-c.)
Arnold, Malcolm. Quintet. Paterson 1961. 2111 (trpt I: c♯'''; trpt II:
    c'''; hn: a♭''; trb: b'; tba: d') (c.)
Bachmann, Fritz, comp. Lass dir unser Lob gefallen. Rufer 1950. 144 p.
    5-part settings: 3(C)020 (j.h.-c.)   score only
Baron, Samuel. Impressions of a Parade, Based on "When Johnny Comes
    Marching Home Again." GSchirmer 1954. 2111 (trpt I: a''; trb:
    a') (h.s.)
Bazelon, Irwin. Brass Quintet (1963). Boosey 1965. 2(C)120 (trpt I:
    d'''; trpt II: c♯'''; hn: c'''; trb I: c♯''; trb II: f♯') (c.)
Beethoven-Ross. Prayer, Op. 48, No. 1. Kendor 1964. 2111/2021 (sub
    trb: g') (j.h.)
Bozza, Eugène. Sonatine. Leduc 1951. 2(C)111 (trpt I: c'''; trpt
    II: b''; hn: a''; trb: b'; tba: g') (c.)
—————. Suite (1967). [MBQ 1967]. 2(C)111 (trpt I: d'''; trpt
    II: b''; hn: b♭''; trb: b'; tba: a') (c.)
—————. Suite française. Leduc 1967. 2(C)111 (trpt I: b''; trpt II:
    g♯''; hn: b''; trb: d''; tba: g') (c.)
Brade, William. 2 Pieces (Hamburg 1609). (R. King) RKing 1961.
    2030/2120/2210-opt tba (trpt I: a''; trb I: a'; trb II: g')
    (j.h.-c.)
Brahms-Rosenthal. 3 Chorale Preludes. Los Angeles, Artransa (WIM)
    1967. 2111 (trpt I: a''; trb: g'; tba: b♭) (j.h.-c.)
Calvert, Morley. Suite from the Monteregian Hills. MBQ n.d. 2111
    (trpts I & II: c'''; trb: a'; tba: d♯') (h.s.-c.) parts only
Childs, Barney. Variations sur une chanson de canotier. Ensemble
    (previously MBQ) 1965. 2111 (trpts I & II: c'''; hn: b♭''; trb:
    c♯''; tba b♭) (c.)
Cobine, Albert. Trilogy for Brass. Ensemble (previously MBQ) 1966.
    2111 (trpt I: f♭'''; trpt II: d'''; hn: a♭''; trb: a'; tba:
    c') (c.)
Coleman, Charles. 4 Pieces for Sackbuts and Cornetts (ca. 1661). (A.
    Baines) Oxford 1960. 2030 (trpt I: a''; trb I: a') (c.)
Dahl, Ingolf. Music for Brass Instruments (1944). Witmark 1949.
    2120-opt tba (trpt I: c♯'''; trpt II: c'''; hn; a''; trb I: b♭';
    trb II: a') (c.)
de Kruyf, Ton. Aubade (1957, rev. 1967). Donemus 1967. 2(C)111
    (trpts I & II, hn: b''; trb: c''; tba: g') (c.)
East, Michael. Desperavi; Fancie. (A. Fromme) AMP 1967. 2120
    (trpts I & II: a''; trb I: a♭') (c.)
Ehmann, Wilhelm, comp. & ed. Alte Spielmusik für Bläser. BVK 1964.
    88 p. 5-part settings: 3(C)020, 2(C)030 (c.) (5-part works by
    M. Praetorius, V. Haussmann, M. Franck, J. H. Schein) score only

————. Bläser-Intraden zum Wochenlied. BVK 1957. 127 p. 5-part
settings: 3020, 2030 (h.s.-c.) score only

Etler, Alvin. Quintet (1963). AMP 1967. 2111 (trpt I: e♭''' ; trpt
II: c''' ; hn: c''' ; trb: d♯'' ; tba: a') (c.)

Eval'd, Victor. Quintet, Op. 5. Ensemble n.d. 2 cts, Althorn, Tenorhorn,
tba (ct I: c''' ; E♭ alto hn: a♭'' ; ten hn: g♭' ; tba: c') (R. King,
as Symphony for Brass Choir) RKing 1957. 2110-bar-opt tba
(trpt I: c''' ; trb & bar: g♭') (h.s.-c.)

Frackenpohl, Arthur. Brass Quintet. Elkan-V 1966. 2111 (trpt I: d''' ;
trb: a♭') (c.)

Gabrieli, Giovanni. Canzona prima a 5. (A. Fromme) CML 1961.
2030/2021/2111/2120 (trb I: g' ; sub tba: b♭) (h.s.-c.)

Gesualdo-Freedman. 4 Madrigals. Toronto, Leeds Music (Canada)
1964. 2111/2021/2030/2120 (h.s.-c.)

Harris, Arthur. 4 Moods (1957). Mentor 1960. 2111 (trpt I: c''' ;
trpt II: b'' ; hn: a♭'' ; trb: b♭' ; tba: g♭) (c.)

Hartley, Walter S. Divertissement (1965). Ensemble 1966. 2111 (trpt
I: c''' ; trpt II: b'' ; trb: b♭' ; tba: c') (h.s.-c.)

————. Quintet (1963). Tenuto 1963. 2111 (trpts I & II: b♭'' ;
hn: a'' ; trb: a' ; tba: a) (h.s.-c.)

Holborne, Anthony. 2 Pieces (London 1599). (R. King) RKing n.d.
2120/2030/1220-opt tba (sub trb: g') (j.h.-c.)

————. 3 Pieces (London 1599). (J. Glasel) CML 1960. 2111/2021
(trpt I: a'' ; trb, sub trb: g' ; tba: c') (c.)

————. 5 Pieces (London 1599). (R. King) RKing 1961. 2120/
2030/2210-opt tba (trpts I & II: a'' ; sub trb: g') (j.h.-c.)

Hübschmann, Werner. Musik. Halle (Saale), Mitteldeutscher Verlag,
1952. 2(C)030 (trb I: a' ; trb II: g') (c.)

Huggler, John. Quintet. CML 1963. 2111 (trpt I: d♯''' ; trpt II:
a'' ; hn: b'' ; trb: a' ; tba: e♭') (c.)

Jones, Collier. 4 Movements for 5 Brass (1957). Mentor 1965. 2111/
2120 (trpt: c''' ; hn: a'' ; trb I: g' ; trb II/tba: g') (h.s.-c.)

Locke, Matthew. Music for His Majesty's Sackbuts and Cornetts (1661).
(A. Baines) Oxford 1951. 2030 (trb I: b♭') (c.)

Maurer, Ludwig. 3 Pieces. (R. Nagel) Mentor 1960. 2210/2120/2111
(trpt I: a'' ; sub trb: g') (h.s.-c.)

————. Scherzo and Lied. (R. Nagel) Mentor 1961. 2210/2120/2111
(trpt I: a'' ; sub trb: a') (j.h.-c.)

Pezel, Johann. Fünff-stimmigte blasende Music (Frankfurt/Main 1685).
(K. Schlegel) Merseburger 1960. score only (A. Lumsden)
MRara 1960. score and parts A selection of Six Pieces and one of
Three Pieces are published by RKing 1955. usually 2120 (usually
trpt I: a'') (j.h.-c.)

————. Hora decima (Leipzig 1670). (A. Lumsden) MRara 1967.
score and parts Single sonatas: (R. King) RKing (2, 3, 22, 25);
(J. Menken – S. Baron) Boosey (5); (N. Greenberg) Mills (12, 28);

(L. Brown) Rubank (27). usually 2120 or 2111 (usually trpt I:
  b♭ ́ ́) (j.h.-c.)
Purcell-Corley. Voluntary on Old 100th. RKing 1957. 2120/2030/2210-
  opt tba (trpt I: a ́ ́ ; sub trb: c ́ ́ ; trb I: g ́) (j.h.-c.)
Purcell [i.e. Clarke]-Corley. Trumpet Voluntary. RKing 1955. 2120/
  3020/3110-opt tba (trpt I: a ́ ́) (j.h.-h.s.)
Roberts, Wilfred. Dixie. Cor 1961. 2111 (j.h.-h.s.)
―――――. 3 Headlines. Cor 1960. 2111 (trpt I: a ́ ́) (j.h.-h.s.)
Sanders, Robert. Quintet in B♭. RKing (previously Music Press) 1948.
  2120 (trpt I: a ́ ́) (c.)
Schlemm, Hans Martin, comp. & ed. Lass dir unser Lob gefallen II.
  Merseburger 1962. 351 p. 5-part settings: 3(C)020, 2(C)030
  (j.h.-c.) score only
Schmidt, William. Suite No. 1. Avant 1967. 2111 (trpt I: c ́ ́ ́ ; tba: g)
  (h.s.-c.)
―――――. Variations on a Negro Folk Song. Avant 1959. 2111 (trpt I:
  g♯ ́ ́) (j.h.-c.)
Schuller, Gunther. Music for Brass Quintet (1961). AMP 1962. 2111
  (trpt I: e ́ ́ ́ ; trpt II: c♯ ́ ́ ́ ; hn: c ́ ́ ́ ; trb: b ́ ; tba: e ́) (c.)
Schumann-Williams. 2 Kinderscenen (*sic*) ("Am Kamin," "Ritter vom
  Steckenpferd"), Op. 15, Nos. 8, 9. SouthernSA 1965. 2111/2021
  (trpt I: a ́ ́ ; sub trb: g ́) (h.s.-c.)
Tull, Fisher. Exhibition; Demonstration Piece for Brass Instruments.
  Avant 1964. 2111 (trpt I: c ́ ́ ́ ; II: b♭ ́ ́ ; trb: c ́ ́ ; tba: b♭) (c.)
Whear, Paul. Invocation and Study. RKing 1960. 2120 (trpt I: b♭ ́ ́)
  (h.s.-c.)
Zaninelli, Luigi. Designs. Templeton 1963. 2030/2120/2111 (trpt I:
  b ́ ́ ; trpt II: c♯ ́ ́ ́ ; trb I: b ́ ; trb II: f♯ ́) (c.)
Zindars, Earl. Quintet. RKing 1958. 2111 (trpt I: c♭ ́ ́ ́ ; trb: g ́ ;
  tba: d ́) (c.)

MIXED SEXTETS

Bachmann, Fritz, comp. Lass dir unser Lob gefallen. Rufer 1950. 144 p.
  6-part settings: mostly 3(C)030 (j.h.-c.) score only
Bezanson, Philip. Prelude and Dance. Interlochen 1961. 2121 (trpt I:
  c♯ ́ ́ ́ ; trpt II: c ́ ́ ́ ; hn: b♭ ́ ́ ; trb I: b ́ ; trb II: g♯ ́ ; tba: b♭)
  (c.)
Böhme, Oskar. Sextet in E♭ minor, Op. 30. Witmark 1934. 2111-bar/
  3021 etc. (trpt I & II: c ́ ́ ́ ; trb: b♭ ́ ; bar: a♭ ́ ; tba: b♭) (h.s.-c.)
Brugk, Hans Melchior. Fanfare und Intrade. Noetzel 1959. 3030
  (trpt I: a ́ ́ ; trb I: g ́) (j.h.-h.s.)
Cadow, Paul. Intrada. Osthofen (Rhh.), "Das Bläserschiff," n.d. 2(C)220
  (g.s.-h.s.)
Dart, Thurston, comp. & ed. Suite from the Royal Brass Music of King
  James I. Oxford 1959. 2(C)040, 3(C)030 (trpt I: g ́ ́ /b ́ ́ ;
  trb I & II: f ́ /a ́) (h.s.-c.)

Ehmann,Wilhelm, comp. & ed. Alte Spielmusik für Bläser. BVK 1964. 88 p. 6-part settings: 3(C)030 (h.s.-c.) 6-part works by M. Praetorius, M. Franck, J. Staden)

—————. Bläser-Intraden zum Wochenlied. BVK 1957. 127 p. 6-part settings: mostly 3(C)030 (h.s.-c.) score only

Handel-King. 3 Pieces from The Water Music. RKing 1955. 3210/2220-opt tba (trpt I: c′′′) (j.h. h.s.)

Kroeger, Karl. Canzona III. Tritone 1968. 3030 (trpt I: c♯′′′; trpt II: b′′; trpt III: a♭′′; trb I: b♭′; trb II: g♭′) (c.)

Locke, Matthew. Music for King Charles II. (R. King) RKing 1960. 3120/2220/3030-opt tba (c.)

Pilss, Karl. 4 Fanfaren. Noetzel 1962. 3030-opt tba (trpt I: g′′/b′′; trb I: f′/g′) (j.h.-h.s.)

Schlemm, Hans Martin, comp. & ed. Lass dir unser Lob gefallen II. Merseburger 1962. 351 p. 6-part settings: mostly 3(C)030 (j.h.-c.) score only

Verrall, John. Suite. Bryn Mawr, Pa., Merion Music (Presser) 1956. 2111-bar (j.h.-h.s.)

MIXED SEPTETS

Berezowsky, Nicolai. Brass Suite, Op. 24. Mills 1942. 2221 (trpt I: c′′′/d′′′; trpt II: c♯′′′; hns: b′′; trb I: c′′; trb II: g′; tba: f′) (c.)

Brugk, Hans Melchior. Suite. Noetzel 1959. 3031-timp (trpt I: c′′′; trb I: g′) (j.h.-h.s.)

Buonamente, Giovanni Battista. Sonata (Venice 1636). (R. King) RKing n.d. 2211-bar (trpt I: b♭′′) (h.s.-c.)

Dubois, Pierre Max. 3 Préludes en fanfare. Leduc 1965. 2(C/B♭)221-opt timp (C trpts, hns: b′′; trb I: a♯′; tba: g′) (c.)

Lasso, Orlando di. Providebam dominum. (R. King) RKing n.d. 4030/5020/4210-opt tba (trb I: a♭′) (c.)

Ruggles, Carl. Angels. New Music (April 1943). 4(C)030 (trpt I: b♭′′; trb I: a♭′) (c.)

Scheurer, Rolf. Scherzo. Presser 1956. 2221-timp (trpt I: c′′′; hn I: b♭′′; trb I: b♭′; tba: g) (h.s.-c.)

Seeboth, Max. Suite. Heinrichshofen 1940. 4030 (trpt I: b′′; trb I: a′) (j.h.-h.s.)

MIXED OCTETS

Gabrieli, Giovanni. Canzon primi toni (Venice 1597). (R. King) RKing 1960. 2 x 2020/1210 etc. (trpts I[1] & II[1]: a′′; trbs I[1] & II[1]: g′) (c.)

—————. Canzon septimi toni no. 2 (Venice 1597). (R. King) RKing 2/1958. 2 x 2020/1210 etc. (trb II[2]: g′) (c.)

————. Canzoni 27 & 28 (Venice 1608). (A. Lumsden) MRara 1967. 4040/4220 (trpts I & II: a''; trbs I & II: b♭'; trb III: g') (c.)
————. Sonata pian' e forte (Venice 1597). (F. Stein) Peters 1932. 2240-opt tba (trb I: a') (R. King) RKing 1958. 2060/1520/2050-viola-opt tba etc. (trbs I¹ & I²: a') (c.)
Weinberger, Jaromir. Concerto for the Timpani. AMP 1939. 4040-timp (trb I: g') (h.s.)

MIXED NONETS

Chou Wen-Chung. Soliloquy of a Bhiksuni. Peters 1961. 1431-perc(3) (trpt: c''') (c.)
Riegger, Wallingford. Nonet for Brass, Op. 49. AMP 1951. 3231 (trpt I: c'''; trpt II: b♭''; trpt III: a''; hn I: a♭''; trb I: b♭'; trb II: a♭'; tba: e♭') (c.)

BASS CHOIR

Arnell, Richard. Ceremonial and Flourish. AMP 1948. 3(C/B♭)430 (B♭ trpt I: c'''/d'''; B♭ trpt II: c'''; B♭ trpt III: a'') (h.s.-c.)
Barnes, Clifford P., comp. & arr. Robbins Collection of Music for Brass Choir. New York, Robbins, 1958. 3431-bar-timp-perc (h.s.)
Beadell, Robert. Introduction and Allegro. RKing 1952. 3331-bar-timp (trpts I & II: d'''; trpt III: b''; hns I & II: a''; tba: g♯) (c.)
Beversdorf, Thomas. Cathedral Music. SouthernSA 1966. 3431-bar (trpts I & II: c'''; trpt III: g♯''; hn I: b♭''; hn III: b''; trb I: a'; trb II: a♭'; bar: g'; tba: g) (h.s.-c.)
Castérède, Jacques. 3 Fanfares pour des proclamations de Napoléon. Leduc 1954. 3(C)431-timp-perc(2)-narrator (trpt I: c'''; trpt II: a♭''; hns: a''; trb I: d♭''; trb II: a'; trb III: g'; tba: f♯') (c.)
Cobine, Albert. Vermont Suite. RKing 1957. 4341-bar (trpts I & II: c'''; trpts III & IV: a''; hns I & II: a''; hn III: b♭''; trb I: c''; trb II: a'; trbs III & IV: g'; tba: g) (h.s.-c.)
Copland, Aaron. Fanfare for the Common Man. Boosey 1944, 1956. 3431-timp-perc (trpts: c'''; hns: b♭''; trb I: b♭'; trb II: g') (h.s.-c.)
Debussy, Claude. Fanfares from "Le Martyre de Saint-Sébastien." Durand 1911. 4(C)631-timp (trpts I & II: b♭''; trb I: g') (c.)
Diamond, David. Ceremonial Fanfare (1950). SouthernNY 1962. 4(C)631-timp(2)-perc(3) (trpts I & II: b''; trpts III & IV: a''; hns I & III: a♯''; hns II, IV, V: a''; trbs I & II: a') (c.)
Dukas, Paul. Fanfare pour précéder "La Péri." Durand 1927. 3(C)431 (hns I & III: a♭''; trb I: a') (h.s.-c.)

Gabrieli, Giovanni. Canzon duodecimi toni (Venice 1597). (R. King) RKing 1958. 2 x 2120/3020/2210-opt tba (trpts I¹ & I²: a''; trbs I¹ & I²: g') (c.)

Hartley, Walter S. Sinfonia No. 3 (1963). Tenuto 1966. 5431-bar (trpt I: b♭''; trpts II & III: a''; hns I & III: b♭''; trb I: b♭'; bar: g♭') (h.s.-c.)

Hartmeyer, John. Negev, Tone Poem for Brass. RKing 1951. 3331-bar-timp (trpt I: c♯'''; trpts II & III: b''; hn I: a♭''; trb I: c♯''; trb II: g♯') (h.s.-c.)

Haufrecht, Herbert. Symphony. Boosey 1967. 3431-timp (trpt I: c'''; trpt II: b''; hn I: b♭''; trb I: c''; trb II: a'; tba: c'/e♭') (h.s.-c.)

Holmes, Paul. Suite for Brass. Shawnee 1960. 3431 (trpt I: c♯'''; trpts II & III: a''; hns: a''; trb I: b'; trb II: g'; tba: g) (h.s.-c.)

Jesson, Roy. Variations and Scherzo. RKing 1954. 4331-bar-timp-sn dr (trpts I-III: b''; trpt IV: a''; hn I: b♭''; hn II: a''; hn III: a♭''; trb I: a'; trb II: g'; tba: a) (c.)

Kauffmann, Leo Justinus. Musik. (K. Janetzky) HofL 1957. 3(C)431 (trpt I: a''; trb I: a'; tba: g) (h.s.-c.)

King, Robert. 7 Conversation Pieces. RKing n.d. 4031-bar(2) (trpts I-III: a''; trb I: g'; bars I & II: a♭') (h.s.-c.)

Marks, James. Music for Brass and Timpani. RKing 1954. 3431-bar-timp (trpt I: d'''; trpt II: b''; trpt III: a♭''; hns: a♭''; trb I: g'; bar: a'; tba: b) (c.)

Merilainen, Usko. Partita. RKing 1959. 4431 (trpts I & III: d'''; trpt II: c'''; hn I: a♭''; trb I: b'; tba: e') (c.)

Merriman, Thomas. Theme and 4 Variations. AMP 1951. 4231-bar (trpt I: d'''; trpt II: c'''; trpt III: b♭''; trpt IV: a''; hns: b♭''; trb I: b♭'; trbs II & III, bar: a') (c.)

Purcell-Smith. Symphony from the Fairy Queen, Act IV. RKing 1957. 6240/6060-timp-opt tba (trpts I & II: c'''; trpt IV: a''; trb I: g') (h.s.-c.)

Purcell [i.e. Clarke]-Brown. Trumpet Voluntary. Summy-B 1958. 4231-bar (trpts solo & I: a'') (h.s.)

Rautavaara, Eino. A Requiem in Our Time. RKing 1958. 4431-bar-timp-perc (trpt I: c'''; trpt II: b''; trpt III: a♭''; hns I-III: b''; hn IV: b♭''; trb I: a♯'; trb II & bar: a') (c.)

Read, Gardner. Sound Piece, Op. 82. RKing 1950. 4432-bar-timp perc(3) (trpt I: c♯'''; trpt II: b♭''; trpt III: c'''; trpt IV: a''; hns I & III: g♯''; trb I: g♯') (c.)

Scott, Wayne. Rondo giojoso. RKing 1956. 3441-bar-timp-perc(2) (trpt I: b''; trb I: b♭'; bar: a♭') (c.)

Tomasi, Henri. Fanfares liturgiques. Leduc 1952. 3(C)431-timp-perc(2) (trpt I: c'''; trpts II & III: a♯''; hn I: c'''; hns II & III: b''; hn IV: opt a♯''; trb I: c♯''; trb II: a'; tba: a) (c.)

Tull, Fisher. Soundings. Templeton 1967. 6642-bar(2)-timp-perc(3)

(trpts I & II: c♯''''; trpt III: a''; trpt IV: g♯''; trpts V & VI:
　　c'''; hns I-VI: a♭''; trbs I & II: a♭'; bar I: g'; tba I: g)
　　(h.s.-c.)

Zindars, Earl. The Brass Square. RKing 1955. 4431-timp-cym (trpts
　　I & II: c'''; trpts III & IV: a''; hn I: g♯''; trbs I & II: g')
　　(h.s.-c.)

TRUMPET SOLOS

Addison, John. Concerto. Williams 1951. (d''') (c.)

Ahlgrimm, Hans. Konzert (1938). Berlin, R. Lienau, 1939. (d''') (c.)

Albrechtsberger, Johann Georg. Concertino in E-flat major. (**R. King**)
　　RKing 1968 (E♭: c''') (c.)

Anderson, Leroy. Bugler's Holiday. Mills 1954. (c''') (j.h.-h.s.)

—————. The Music of Leroy Anderson. Mills 1962. 40 p. (Blue Tango,
　　Promenade, The Syncopated Clock, Song of the Bells, Forgotten
　　Dreams, The First Day of Spring, Saraband, The Phantom Regi-
　　ment) (j.h.-h.s.)

—————. A Trumpeter's Lullaby. Mills 1950. (a'') (j.h.-h.s.)

Antheil, George. Sonata. New York, Weintraub Music Co., 1953.
　　(c♯'''/d''') (c.)

Arban, J. J. B. L. The Carnival of Venice; Fantaisie and Variations.
　　Cundy-B n.d. (h.s.-c.)

Arnell, Richard. Trumpet Allegro, Op. 58, No. 2. SchottL 1952. C/B♭
　　(B♭: b'') (h.s.-c.)

Arutunian, A. Concerto. HofL 1954. (b♭'') (c.)

Asafiev, Boris. Sonata (1939). (W. Beeler) Leeds 1951. (c''') (c.)

Aubain, Jean Emmanuel. Marche et scherzo. Leduc 1958. C/B♭
　　(C: c♭''') (h.s.-c.)

Baines, Francis. Pastoral. SchottL 1952. (c''') (h.s.-c.)

Beeler, Walter, comp. & arr. Solos for the Trumpet Player. GSchirmer
　　1963. 83 p. (h.s.-c.) (works by Adam, J. S. Bach, Balay, Bizet,
　　de Fesch, Gautier, Handel, Haydn, Marais, Massenet, Mozart,
　　Rameau, Ropartz, Schubert, and Senaillé)

Benson, Warren. Prologue. Piedmont 1959. (g.s.-j.h.)

Berghmans, José. La Chenille. Leduc 1958. C/B♭ (C: a'') (h.s.-c.)

Bernstein, Leonard. Rondo for Lifey. GSchirmer 1950. (c''') (h.s.-c.)

Biber, Heinrich Ignaz Franz. Sonata a 6. (K. Janetzky) MRara 1958.
　　trpt, strings, bc (c''') (c.)

Blum, Robert. Capriccio (1959). Henn-C n.d. (C: c''') (c.)

Böhme, Oskar. Concerto in F minor, Op. 18. (F. Herbst) Hamburg,
　　D. Rahter, 1941. (d''') (c.)

Bohrnstedt, Wayne. Concerto. Remick 1953. (d♭''') (c.)

Booren, Jo van den. Game III (1966). Donemus 1966. trpt in C, organ
　　(c.)

Brandt, W. Concertpiece, Op. 12. (R. Nagel) IMC 1960. (b♭'')
(h.s.-c.)

Brenta, Gaston. Concertino. Leduc 1958. (C: d'''/e''') (c.)

Breuer, Karl G. Atonalyse II. Sikorski 1959. trpt in C, strings (a'')
(h.s.-c.)

Brun, François Julien. Promenade. Leduc 1958. C/B♭ (C: a♭'')
(h.s.-c.)

Cabus, P. Rondo ostinato. Maurer 1967. (a'') (j.h.-h.s.)

Canty, Daniel J., comp. Bugle Signals, Calls and Marches. Ditson (Presser) 1916. 68 p. (j.h.-h.s.)

Castérède, Jacques. Sonatine. Leduc 1956. (C: a♯''/e♭''') (c.)

Challan, Henri. Variations. Leduc 1959. (C: b'') (c.)

Chaynes, Charles. Concerto. Leduc 1956. (C: c♯''') (c.)

Childs, Barney. Interbalances IV (1962). Tritone 1962. unacc trpt,
opt narrator (c''', more or less) (c.)

Clérisse, Robert. Noce villageoise. Leduc 1959. C/B♭ (j.h.-h.s.)

–––––. Thème varié. Leduc 1959. C/B♭ (j.h.-h.s.)

Cole, Hugo. The Hammersmith Galop. SchottL 1952. C/B♭ (B♭: a'')
(h.s.-c.)

Constant, Marius. 3 Mouvements. Leduc 1960. C/B♭ (B♭: c''') (c.)

Contemporary French Recital Pieces. IMC 1954. (C: g''-c''')
(h.s.-c.) (works by Ameller, Cushing, Jolivet, Lesur, Pascal, and
Semenoff)

Croley, Randell. Variazioni (1965). Tritone 1968. unacc (d♭''') (c.)

Désenclos, A. Incantation, Thrène et Danse. Leduc 1953. (C: c♯''')
(c.)

Eckard, Walter, comp. & arr. 12 Program Solos. Presser 1955. 46 p.
(j.h.-h.s.) (works by Handel, Borodin, Mussorgsky, Stravinsky,
and Prokofiev)

Enesco, Georges. Legend. IMC n.d. C/B♭ (C: c''') (c.)

Fasch, Johann Friedrich. Concerto in D major. (H. Winschermann-F.
Buck) Sikorski 1964. (D: d''') (c.)

Fitzgerald, R. Bernard. English Suite. Presser 1955. (j.h.-h.s.)

Flothuis, Marius. Aria, Op. 18 (1944). Donemus 1947. (C: f♯'')
(h.s.-c.)

Frackenpohl, Arthur. Sonatina . . . Based on Two Sonatinas by Friedrich
Kuhlau. GSchirmer 1964. (c''') (h.s.)

Françaix, Jean. Sonatine. Eschig 1952. (C: c''') (c.)

Friboulet, Georges. Introduction et marche. Lemoine 1958. (C: c''')
(j.h.-h.s.)

Gabaye, Pierre. Boutade. Leduc 1957. C/B♭ (C: a'') (j.h.-h.s.)

–––––. Sonatine. Leduc 1961. C/B♭ (C: c''') (c.)

Gabrielli, Domenico. 6 Sonatas. (R. Voisin) IMC 1967. (C: a''/c''')
(c.)

Gallois Montbrun, Raymond. Lied. Leduc 1950. C/B♭ (B♭: a'')
(h.s.)

————. Marche. Leduc 1950. C/B♭ (C: a ' ') (h.s.)

————. Scherzo. Leduc 1950. C/B♭ (B♭: a ' ') (h.s.)

Gershwin-Sauter. Gershwin for Trumpet. Harms 1952. 32 p. (h.s.)

Giannini, Vittorio. Concerto. Remick 1948. (c ' ' ') (c.)

Glasenapp, Franz von, and Erwin Wolf, comp. & arr. Rostocker Suite nach Trompetenmusik des 18. Jahrhunderts. HofL 1956. (c ' ' ') (h.s.-c.)

Glière-Findlay. 2 Pieces (Meditation, Op. 34, No. 21; Mazurka, Op. 43, No. 3). Leeds 1958. (b♭ ' ') (j.h.-h.s.)

Goedicke, Alexander. Concert Etude, Op. 49. Leeds 1946. (b♭ ' ') (h.s.-c.)

Gould-Edwards. Pavanne. Mills 1944. (b♭ ' ') (j.h.-h.s.)

Hamilton, Iain. Capriccio. SchottL 1952. (b ' ') (c.)

Handel-Musser. Concerto. Fox 1962. (a ' ') (h.s.)

————. Sonata. Fox 1963. (h.s.)

Hartley, Walter. Sonatina. Rochester Music Pubrs., 1956. (c ' ' ') (h.s.-c.)

Haydn, Franz Joseph. Concerto in E♭ major. (E. Hall) Boosey 1945. (e♭ ' ' ') (c.)

Haydn, Johann Michael. Concerto in D major. (W. Haseke) Simrock 1965. (D: g ' ' ') (c.)

Hindemith, Paul. Sonate (1939). SchottM 1940. (b ' ') (c.)

Hoddinott, Alun. Rondo scherzoso, Op. 12, No. 1. Oxford 1958. (d ' ' ') (c.)

Honegger, Arthur. Intrada. Salabert 1947. (C: c ' ' ') (c.)

Hovhaness, Alan. Prayer of Saint Gregory. Peer 1952. trpt, strings; trpt, pf/organ (b ' ') (j.h.-h.s.)

Hummel, Johann Nepomuk. Concerto in E♭ major. (A. Ghitalla) RKing 1959. trpt, pf; trpt, band (c ' ' ') (h.s.-c.)

Ibert, Jacques. Impromptu (1951). Leduc 1951. (C: c ' ' ') (c.)

Johnson, Clair W., comp. & arr. Sacred Solos. Rubank 1960. 51 p. (j.h.-h.s.)

Kennan, Kent. Sonata. Remick 1956. (c ' ' ') (c.)

Ketting, Otto. Intrada (1958). Donemus 1958. unacc trpt/hn (b♭ ' ') (c.)

Kinyon, John, comp. & arr. Breeze-Easy Recital Pieces. Witmark 1958. 32 p. (g.s.-j.h.)

Korda, Viktor. Sonatine. Doblinger 1964. (c ' ' ') (c.)

Krebs, Johann Ludwig. 8 Chorale Preludes. (E. P. Biggs) Mercury 1947. C/B♭ trpt, organ (h.s.-c.)

Lantier, Pierre. Concert en trois parties. Lemoine 1957. (C: c ' ' ') (c.)

Lawton, Sidney M. The Young Trumpet-Player. Oxford 1959. 3 vols. (16, 13, 16 p.) (g.s.-h.s.)

Legley, Victor. Sonata, Op. 40, No. 6 (1953). CeBeDeM 1956. (C: a ' ') (c.)

McKay, George F. Concert Solo Suite for Young Players. CFischer 1962. (g.s.)

Mayer, William. Concert Piece. Boosey 1959. (c′′′) (c.)

Meyer, Lawrence J., comp. & arr. 15 Folk Tunes. Shawnee 1966. 23 p. (g.s.-j.h.)

Molter, Johann Melchior. Concerto in D major. (M. Rasmussen) RKing 1969. (D: d′′′) (c.)

Nelhybel, Vaclav. Suite. General 1966. (j.h.)

Oboussier, Robert. Entrada (1943). Lausanne, M. & P. Foetisch, 1952. (C: c′′′) (c.)

Pakhmutova, Alexandra. Concerto (1955). GMI, Leeds, 1959. (d♭′′′) (c.)

Persichetti, Vincent. The Hollow Men. Elkan-V 1948. trpt, strings; trpt, pf/organ (c♯′′′) (c.)

Pilss, Karl. Sonate (1935). Universal 1962. (b′′/c′′′) (c.)

Presser, William. Suite. Kendor 1964. (c′′′) (j.h.-h.s.)

Prokofiev-Maganini. Kije's Wedding. EMusicus 1944. (a′′) (j.h.-h.s.)

Purcell, Henry. Sonata in D major. (A. Ghitalla) RKing 1960, 1963. trpt, organ; trpt, strings, bc (c♯′′′) (A. Lumsden) MRara 1962. trpt, strings, bc (D: a′′) (c.)

Raphael, Günter. Marche. Leduc 1959. (c′′′) (h.s.-c.)

Raymond, Lewis. Design. Avant 1965. (a′′) (h.s.-c.)

Riisager, Knudage. Concertino, Op. 29. Hansen 1935. trpt, pf; trpt, strings (c′′′) (c.)

Rohlig, Harald. 8 Intradas and Chorales. Concordia 1959. trpt, organ (a′′/b′′) (h.s.-c.)

Sanders, Robert L. Square Dance. Galaxy 1959. (b♭′′/c′′′) (j.h.-h.s.)

Schmitt, Florent. Suite, Op. 133. Durand 1955. (C: d′′′) (c.)

Schneider, Willy, comp. & arr. Little Pieces by Old Masters. SchottM 1961. 14 p. (j.h.) (works by Schein, Lully, de Fesch, Fux, Telemann, Purcell, Daquin, Beethoven, and Anon.)

Schröter, Heinz. Fanfarette. Leduc 1963. unacc (a′′) (h.s.-c.)

Seeboth, Max. Sonate. Noetzel 1963. (b′′) (c.)

Shapero, Harold. Sonata (1940). SouthernNY 1956. (C: b′′) (c.)

Stanley-Coleman. Trumpet Tune. Oxford 1960. B♭ trpt, pf; C trpt, strings (B♭: a′′) (j.h.-c.)

Starer, Robert. Invocation. Mills 1962. (c′′′) (h.s.-c.)

Stevens, Halsey. Sonata. Peters 1959. (d′′′) (c.)

Stradella, Alessandro. Sonata. (O. Jander) RKing 1960. trpt, strings (c♯′′′) (c.)

Telemann, Georg Philipp. Concerto in D major. (K. Grebe) Sikorski 1959. trpt, pf; trpt, strings (D: d′′′) (c.)

————. 20 Excerpts from 12 Fantasien für Querflöte (1735). (W. Roché) n.p., Rochemont, n.d. unacc (a′′/e′′′) (c.)

————. Heldenmusik. (E. Pätzold) IMC 1956. (b♭′′/d′′′) (j.h.-c.)

Tomasi, Henri. Triptyque. Leduc 1957. C/B♭ (B♭: d′′′) (c.)

Torelli, Giuseppe. Sinfonia con tromba. (J. Berger) RKing 1958. trpt, organ; trpt, strings (c♯′′′) (c.)
Weber, Alain. Strophes. Leduc 1966. (C: c′′′) (c.)
White, Donald H. Sonata. RKing 1967. (c′′′/d′′′) (c.)
Wissmer, Pierre. Concertino (1959). Henn-C n.d. (C: c′′′) (c.)

*

Bergese, Hans, comp. & ed. Alte und neue Tänze. SchottM n.d. 40 p. rec, opt hand drum (g.s.-j.h.)
Buxtehude, Dietrich. Choralvorspiele. (F. Jöde) Moeck 1948. rec, organ/pf (C: g′′/e′′′) (c.)
Degen, Dietz, comp. & ed. Fröhliche Jagd. BVK [pref. 1939]. 1-2 rec (g.s.-j.h.)
Diabelli, Antonio. Sonata in C (arr. from Op. 163). (W. Bergmann) SchottL 1962. rec, pf (j.h.-h.s.)
Eyck, Jacob van. Der Fluyten Lust-hof (Amsterdam 1646). (G. Vellekoop) Amsterdam, Ixijzet, 1957. 3 vols. unacc rec (a′′/c′′′) (c.)
Fegers, Karl. 8 Tanzmelodien (1962). Moeck 1964. (Zs. für Spielmusik 298) rec, pf (C: e′′/a′′) (j.h.)
Finger, Godfrey. Sonata. (W. Bergmann) SchottL 1962. rec, pf (C: g′′) (j.h.-h.s.)
Fischer, Johann. Suite in G (Dresden 1699/1700). (W. Bergmann) SchottL 1952. rec, pf (C: b′′) (c.)
Fischer, (Johann) Kaspar Ferdinand. Spielstücke (from Le Journal de printemps, Augsburg 1695). (W. Woehl) BVK [pref. 1937]. 2 vols. rec, pf (C: e′′/g′′) (j.h.-c.)
Frei, Walter, comp. & ed. Mittelalterliche Spielmannsmusik. BVK 1960. unacc rec (g.s.-j.h.)
Frescobaldi, Girolamo. Canzona (Venice 1634). (C. Sterne) Galaxy 1965. rec, bc (C: a′′) (h.s.-c.)
Holst, Imogen, comp. & ed. 100 Traditional Irish Tunes. Boosey 1955. unacc rec (f′′/b♭′′) (g.s.-j.h.)
Hook, James. Sonata in G (arr. from Op. 99) (London ca.1800). (W. Bergmann) SchottL 1948. rec, pf (C: e′′) (j.h.-h.s.)
Hunt, Edgar H., comp. & ed. 50 Old English Folk-Dance Airs. SchottL 1939. unacc rec (d′′/c′′′) (g.s.-j.h.)
Kodály, Zoltán. Epigrams. (P. M. Young) Boosey 1963. voice, pf (j.h.-h.s.)
Lechner, Konrad. Volkslied-Improvisationen. BVK 1960. unacc rec (d′′/b′′) (j.h.-h.s.)
Marx, Karl. Flötenbüchlein für Klaus (1950). BVK 2/1964. rec, pf (C: d′′/a′′) (g.s.-j.h.)
Schneider, Willy, comp. & arr. Flötenbüchlein für einsame Spieler. Noetzel 1956. unacc rec (g.s.-j.h.)
Strungk, Nicolaus Adam. Suiten und Airs. (D. Degen) Peters 1943. rec, bc (C: a′′/c′′′) (c.)

Telemann, Georg Philipp. Ausgewählte Menuette. (W. Woehl) BVK
  [pref. 1936]. rec, pf (C: f''/a'') (h.s.-c.)
————. 15 Stücke aus "Sieben mal sieben und ein Menuette" (1728).
  (E. Pätzold) Lienau 1949. fl, bc (C: g''/c''') (h.s.-c.)

HORN SOLOS

Akimenko, Feodor. Melody. Leeds 1945. (a'') (j.h.-h.s.)
Apostel, Hans Erich. Sonatine, Op. 39b. Universal 1965. unacc (c''')
  (c.)
Bassett, Leslie. Sonata. RKing (previously E. H. Morris) 1954. (b'')
  (c.)
Beethoven, Ludwig van. Sonata in F major, Op. 17. Peters n.d. (M.
  Wolff) Boosey 1949. (c.)
Benson, Warren. Soliloquy. Piedmont 1959. (f'') (g.s.-j.h.)
Bentzon, Niels Viggo. Sonata, Op. 47. Hansen 1950. (c''') (c.)
Bernstein, Leonard. Elegy for Mippy I. GSchirmer 1950. (b''/c''')
  (h.s.-c.)
Bozza, Eugène. Chant lointain. Leduc 1957. (g♯'') (c.)
Butterworth, Arthur. Romanza. Hinrichsen 1960. hn, pf; hn, strings
  (b♭'') (c.)
Butterworth, Neil. Prelude and Scherzo. Chappell 1961. (j.h.-h.s.)
Capdevielle, Pierre. Élégie de Duino. Leduc 1960. (c''') (c.)
Chabrier, Emmanuel. Larghetto. Costallat (Salabert) 1913. hn, pf
  (a'') (c.) (Froseth) Park Ridge, Ill., N. Kjos, 1962. hn,
  woodwind ensemble
Cherubini, Luigi. 2 Sonaten. (J. Wojciechowski) Sikorski 1954. hn,
  pf; hn, strings (a'') (c.)
Childs, Barney. Variations for David Racusen. Tritone 1967. unacc
  (b'') (c.)
Clérisse, Robert. L'Absent. Leduc 1957. (j.h.-h.s.)
Cooke, Arnold. Rondo in B♭. SchottL 1952. (h.s.-c.)
Corrette, Michel. Concerto in C major, "La Choisy." (E. Leloir) Hein-
  richshofen 1967. (h.s.-c.)
Danzi, Franz. Sonata in E♭ major, Op. 28. (G. Hausswald) HofL 1958.
  hn in E♭, pf (c.)
————. Sonate concertante, Op. 44. (J. Wojciechowski) Sikorski 1957.
  hn in E, pf (c.)
Donato, Anthony. Sonata. Remick 1950. (a'') (c.)
Dubois, Pierre Max. A cor et a cri. Leduc 1966. (g'') (g.s.-j.h.)
Dukas, Paul. Villanelle. Durand 1906. (a''/c''') (c.) (also in
  Jones)
Eder, Helmut. Sonatine, Op. 34, No. 6. Doblinger 1966. (a'') (c.)
Eyck, Jacob van. Der Fluyten Lust-hof (Amsterdam 1646). (G. Velle-
  koop) Amsterdam, Ixijzet, 1957. 3 vols. unacc rec (a''/c''')
  (c.)

Françaix, Jean. Canon in octave. IMC 1953. (j.h.-h.s.)

Gipps, Ruth. Sonatina, Op. 56. Fox 1961. (g.s.-j.h. — 2d mvt only)

Glazunov, Alexander. Reverie, Op. 24. Leeds 1945. (a♭ʹʹ) (j.h.-c.) (also in Jones)

Glière, Reinhold. Concerto, Op. 91. (J. Singer) Leeds 1957. (a♯ʹʹ) (c.)

————. Intermezzo, Op. 35, No. 11. Leeds 1947. (j.h.-c.)

————. Nocturne, Op. 35, No. 10. Leeds 1945. (j.h.-c.)

Grudzinski, Czeslaw. Miniatury. PWM 1964. (j.h.-h.s.)

Guarnieri, M. Camargo. Etude (1953). Rongwen 1958. (cʹʹʹ) (c.)

Hamilton, Iain. Aria. SchottL 1952. (aʹʹ) (c.)

Haydn, Franz Joseph. Concerto No. 1 in D major. (H. H. Steves) Boosey 1952. D/F (D: dʹʹʹ) (c.)

————. Concerto No. 2 in D major. (H. H. Steves) Boosey 1953. D/F (D: aʹʹ) (c.)

Haydn, Johann Michael. Romance. (M. Rasmussen) RKing 1968. hn in E♭, pf; hn, strings (h.s.-c.)

Heiden, Bernhard. Sonata (1939). AMP 1955. (bʹʹ) (c.)

Hindemith, Paul. Concerto (1949). SchottM 1950. (aʹʹ) (c.)

————. Sonate (1939). SchottM 1940. (aʹʹ) (c.)

————. Sonata for Alto Horn in E♭ (1943). SchottM 1956. (E♭: cʹʹʹ) (c.)

Holmes, Paul. Serenade. Shawnee 1962. (aʹʹ) (h.s.-c.)

Hughes, Mark. Sonata. Tritone 1966. (b♭ʹʹ/bʹʹ) (c.)

Jones, Donald R. Allegro. Westbury, N.Y., Pro Art, 1963. (b♭ʹʹ/cʹʹʹ) (h.s.-c.)

Jones, Mason, comp. & ed. Solos for the Horn Player. GSchirmer 1962. 96 p. (j.h.-h.s.) (works by Beethoven, Brahms, Dukas, Frackenpohl, Glazunov, Handel, Labor, Lefebvre, Mendelssohn, Mozart, Purcell, Ravel, Saint-Saëns, Stradella)

Jongen, Joseph. Lied (1899). CeBeDeM 1960. (aʹʹ) (h.s.-c.)

Ketting, Otto. Intrada (1958). Donemus 1958. unacc trpt/hn (b♭ʹʹ) (c.)

Kinyon, John. Breeze-Easy Recital Pieces. Witmark 1958. 32 p. (g.s.-j.h.)

Korn, Peter Jona. Sonate, Op. 18. Simrock 1959. (bʹʹ) (c.)

Krol, Bernhard. Laudatio. Simrock 1966. unacc (b♭ʹʹ) (h.s.-c.)

Kurka, Robert. Ballad, Op. 36. Weintraub 1961. (cʹʹʹ) (c.)

Levy, Frank. Suite. Cor 1961. (gʹʹ/g♯ʹʹ) (j.h.-h.s.)

Meyer, Jean. Cordelinette. Lemoine 1964. (j.h.-h.s.)

Miroshnikov, O. Rondo. GMI 1962. (bʹʹ) (c.)

Mozart, Wolfgang Amadeus. 4 Horn Concertos and Concert Rondo. (H. Kling) Breitkopf n.d. (separate publications) GSchimer 1960. (all in one volume) (f♯ʹʹ/b♭ʹʹ) (c.)

————. Quintet, K. 407 (K.-E.368b). (P. Hodgson) Peters 1963. hn, pf (b♭ʹʹ) (c.)

Nielsen, Carl. Canto serioso. Copenhagen, Skandinavisk Musikforlag, 1944. (c.)

Orr, Robin. Serenade. SchottL 1952. (h.s.-c.)

Poole, Reid. A Song of a City. Belwin 1965. E♭/F (j.h.-h.s.)

Porter, Quincy. Sonata. Chicago, Gamble, 1948. (c''') (c.)

Poser, Hans. Sonate, Op. 8. Sikorski 1957. (a♭'') (c.)

Poulenc, Francis. Elegie (In Memory of Denis Brain) (1957). London, J. & W. Chester, 1958. (a'') (c.)

Presser, William. Fantasy on the Hymn Tune "The Mouldering Vine." Tritone 1963. (b'') (c.)

————. 3 Pieces (1966). Louisville 1966. unacc (b'') (c.)

Ravel, Maurice. Pavane pour une infante défunte. (A. Piguet) Eschig 1913. (a'') (j.h.-c.) (another version in Jones)

Reynolds, Verne. Partita. SouthernSA 1964. (g♯'') (c.)

Rheinberger, Joseph. Sonata in E♭ major, Op. 178. (M. S. Kastner) SchottM 1967. (b♮'') (c.)

Rosetti, F. A. Concerto in D minor. (B. Krol) Simrock 1959. (a'') (c.)

————. Concerto in E♭ major. (J. Chambers) IMC 1960. (E♭: c''') (h.o. o.)

Rossini, Gioacchino. Prélude, Thème et Variations. (D. Ceccarossi) Pesaro, Fondazione Rossini, 1954. (Quaderni Rossiniani III) (g''/c''') (c.)

Rueff, Jeanine. Cantilène. Leduc 1963. (j.h.-h.s.)

Saint-Saëns, Camille. Romance. IMC n.d. (j.h.-h.s.) (also in Jones)

Sanders, Robert. Sonata in B♭ (1958). RKing 1963. (c''') (c.)

Schibler, Armin. Prologue, Invocation et Danse, Op. 47. Berlin, Wiesbaden, Ahn & Simrock, 1956. (b♮'') (c.)

Schmitt, Florent. Lied et Scherzo, Op. 54. Durand 1912. (b♮'') (c.)

Schreiter, Heinz. Sonatine, Op. 12. Berlin, Bote & Bock, 1954. (a'') (c.)

Schumann, Robert. Adagio und Allegro, Op. 70. Peters, IMC, n.d. (c''') (c.)

Scriabine, Alexander. Romance. Leeds 1945. (j.h.-c.)

Shollar, F. Skola Igry na Valtorne. Moscow, Muzgiz, 1955. 152 p. (j.h.-h.s.) O/P

Stevens, Halsey. 4 Short Pieces. Camara 1960. (b♮'') (h.s.-c.)

————. Sonata. RKing (previously E. H. Morris) 1955. (c''') (c.)

Stich, Wenzel. Concerto No. 7 in F major. (A. Gottron) WMüller 1961. (c''') (c.)

Strauss, Franz. Thema und Variationen, Op. 13. Zimmermann 1957. (a♭''/b♮'') (h.s.-c.)

Strauss, Richard. Concerto No. 1 in E♭ major, Op. 11. IMC n.d. (b♮'') (c.)

Telemann, Georg Philipp. Concerto in D major. (E. Leloir) Locarno, Edizioni Pegasus (Peters) 1964. (D: d''') (c.)

Tillotson, Natalie. Fantasy (1959). CML 1962. (a'') (h.s.-c.)
Tomasi, Henri. Danse profane. Leduc 1960. (g♯''/b'') (h.s.-c.)
Vuillermoz, Edouard, arr. Les Classiques du cor. Leduc 1943. (j.h.-h.s.)
  Separately published series, including works by Bach, Grétry, Handel,
  Mendelssohn, Mozart, Schubert, and Schumann.
Weber, Carl Maria von. Concertino in E minor, Op. 45. Breitkopf n.d.
  (E: e''') (c.)
Weigel, Eugene. Maine Sketches. Interlochen n.d. (a♭'') (h.s.-c.)
Wellesz, Egon. Fanfares for Horn Solo, Op. 78. Rongwen 1958. unacc
  (h.s.-c.)
Whear, Paul. Pastorale Lament. Interlochen n.d. (a'') (j.h.-c.)
Wolf, J. E. de. Sonatine in oude stijl. Maurer 1960. (j.h.)
Wolff, Christian. Duet II. Peters 1962. graph notation (c.)

TROMBONE SOLOS

Albrechtsberger, Johann Georg. Concerto in B♭ major. (R. King) RKing
  1969. trb, pf; trb, strings (d'') (c.)
Ameller, André. Kryptos; Etude. Hinrichsen 1958. (b'/c♯'') (c.)
Bach-Beversdorf. Endure! Endure! Air from Passion "St. Matthew."
  SouthernSA 1961. (a') (h.s.)
————. Haste, Ye Shepherds; Air from "Christmas Oratorio." Southern-
  SA 1961. (a') (h.s.)
————. 'Tis Thee I Would be Praising; Air from "Christmas Oratorio."
  SouthernSA 1961. (g') (h.s.)
Barat, J. E. Andante et allegro. Cincinnati, A. J. Andraud (SouthernSA)
  n.d. (b♭') (h.s.)
Bariller, Robert. L'Enterrement de Saint-Jean. Leduc 1960. (j.h.-h.s.)
————. Hans de Schnokeloch. Leduc 1961. (bass trb) (a') (h.s.)
Bassett, Leslie. Sonata. RKing 1967. (c'') (c.)
————. Suite. Louisville 1967. unacc (d'') (c.)
Bavicchi, John. Preludes, Op. 21. Ensemble 1966. unacc (b♭'/c♯'')
  (c.)
Beach, Bennie. Suite. AMP 1957. (g') (c.)
Benson, Warren. Aubade. Piedmont 1959. (g.s.-j.h.)
Bernstein, Leonard. Elegy for Mippy II. GSchirmer 1940. unacc (b♭')
  (c.)
Blazhevich, Vladislav. Concert Sketch No. 5. (R. Satz) Leeds 1946.
  (b♭') (h.s.)
Boda, John. Sonatina. New York, W. D. Stuart Music (RKing) 1963.
  (a') (c.)
Boutry, Roger. Capriccio. Leduc 1957. (c♯'') (c.)
————. Choral varié. Leduc 1956. (a') (h.s.-c.)
————. Concerto. Leduc 1963. (c♯'') (c.)

Cage, John. Solo for Sliding Trombone; Pages 173-184 of the Orchestral Parts of Concert for Piano and Orchestra (1957-58). New York, Henmar Press (Peters) 1960. (d′′, more or less) (c.)

Castérède, Jacques. Fantaisie concertante. Leduc 1960. (bass trb) (a′) (c.)

————. Sonatine. Leduc 1958. (c′′) (c.)

Childs, Barney. Sonata (1961). Tritone 1962. unacc. (d′′/e′′) (c.)

Clérisse, Robert. Prière. Leduc 1959. (f♯′) (h.s.)

Coker, Wilson. Concerto for Tenor-Bass Trombone and Symphonic Band. Presser 1961. trb, pf (c′′) (c.)

Creston, Paul. Fantasy, Op. 42. GSchirmer 1951. (c♯′′/d♯′′) (c.)

Croley, Randell. Variazioni piccola (sic), Op. 44, No. 1. Louisville 1965. unacc bass trb (c′′) (c.)

Daneels, François. Petite pièce. Maurer 1961. (j.h.)

David, Ferdinand. Concertino, Op. 4. (F. Grube) Hamburg, A. J. Benjamin, n.d. (c′′) (c.)

Désenclos, Alfred. Plain-chant et allegretto. Leduc 1965. (c♯′′) (c.)

Dubois, Pierre Max. Cortège. Leduc 1959. (g′) (h.s.)

————. 2 Marches. Leduc 1960. (c′′) (h.s.)

Dubois, Théodore. Concertpiece (Solo de concert). IMC n.d. (c′′) (h.s.-c.)

Fasch, Johann Friedrich. Sonata in C major. (J. Wojciechowski) Litolff 1961. bn, pf (A. Fromme-L. Seeber) McG&M 1961. trb, pf (g′) (c.)

Frackenpohl, Arthur R. Pastorale. Rochester 1952. (a♭′/d♭′′) (c.)

Gabaye, Pierre. Tubabillage. Leduc 1959. (bass trb) (h.s.)

Gagnebin, Henri. Sarabande. Leduc 1953. (j.h.-c.)

Gardner, John. Romanza. SchottL 1952. (g♭′) (c.)

Gräfe, Friedebald. Grand Concerto. Cundy-B n.d. (c′′) (c.)

Guilmant, Alexandre. Concertpiece, Op. 88. IMC n.d. (b♭′/c♯′′) (h.s.-c.) (also in Smith)

Handel-Beversdorf. The Enemy Said; Air from "Israel in Egypt." SouthernSA 1961. (a′) (h.s.)

————. Ev'ry Valley; Air from "Messiah." SouthernSA 1961. (g♯′) (h.s.)

————. From Celestial Seats Descending; Air from "Hercules." SouthernSA 1961. (a′) (h.s.)

Hartley, Walter S. Sonata concertante (1956-58). Interlochen n.d. (c′′) (c.)

Haydn-Beversdorf. And Now Revived He Springs; Air from "The Seasons." SouthernSA 1961. (b′) (h.s.)

Henry, Otto. Passacaglia and Fugue. RKing 1963. (bass trb) (a′) (c.)

Hindemith, Paul. Sonate (1941). SchottM 1942. (b′) (c.)

Hovhaness, Alan. Concerto No. 3; Diran (The Religious Singer). RKing 1962. baritone hn, strings (b♭′) (h.s.-c.)

Hugon, Georges. Introduction et allegro. EMT 1961. (d'') (c.)

Jones, Robert W. Sonatina. Interlochen n.d. (a') (c.)

Kinyon, John, comp. & arr. Breeze-Easy Recital Pieces. Witmark 1958. 32 p. (g.s.-j.h.)

Looser, Rolf. Variationenfantasie über ein eigenes Choralthema (1958). Henn-C 1958. (e♭'') (c.)

Martin, Frank. Ballade (1940). Universal 1941. (d'') (c.)

Mellers, Wilfred. Galliard. SchottL 1952. (b♮') (c.)

Milhaud, Darius. Concertino d'hiver (1953). AMP 1955, 1957. trb, pf; trb, strings (c'') (c.)

Morrissey, John J. Song. Piedmont 1960. (g'/a') (j.h.)

Mullins, Gene, comp. & arr. 12 Easy Classics. Summy-B 1956. 23 p. (j.h.-h.s.) (pieces by Bach, Byrd, Corelli, Gluck, Handel, and Tenaglia)

Perry, Harold, comp. & arr. Classical Album. Boosey 1964. 16 p. (a'/b♭') (h.s.) (pieces by Schubert, Mozart, Handel, Mendelssohn, Chopin, Beethoven, Bach, Purcell)

Presser, William. Sonatina. Tritone 1962. (a') (h.s.-c.)

Reuter, Fritz. Suite, Op. 23. Zimmermann n.d. unacc (b♭') (c.)

Rimsky-Korsakov, Nikolay Andreyevitch. Concerto for Trombone and Band. Leeds 1952. trb, pf; trb, band (b♭') (h.s.-c.)

Roy, Klaus George. Sonata, Op. 13. RKing [1963]. (b♭') (c.)

Salzedo, Carlos. Pièce concertante, Op. 27. IMC n.d. (d♭'') (c.)

Sanders, Robert. Sonata in E♭ major. Chicago, Gamble, 1948. (b♮') (c.)

Schibler, Armin. Signal, Beschwörung und Tanz; Konzert, Op. 55. Berlin, Wiesbaden, Ahn & Simrock, 1959. (c''/d♭'') (c.)

Semler-Collery, Jules. Fantaisie lyrique. Eschig 1960. (c♯'') (c.)

Smith, Henry C., comp. & arr. Solos for the Trombone Player. GSchirmer 1963. 51 p. (h.s.) (pieces by Haydn, Handel, Galliard, Rimsky-Korsakov, Bach, Guilmant, Bernstein, Franck, Corelli, Berlioz, Reiche, Serocki, and Rachmaninoff)

Tanner, Paul. Moods from Dorian. Belwin 1965. (g') (j.h.-h.s.)

Tomasi, Henri. Danse sacrée. Leduc 1960. (a♭') (h.s.-c.)

Trevarthen, R. R. Sonata. Louisville 1966. (c'') (c.)

Wagenseil, Georg Christoph. Concerto in E♭ major. (K. Janetzky) W-Müller 1963. (c'') (c.)

Watson, Walter. Sonatina. Shawnee 1962. (b') (c.)

•

Bach, Johann Christian. Concerto in B♭ major. (J. Wojciechowski) Sikorski 1953. bn, pf (a♭') (c.)

———. Concerto in E♭ major. (J. Wojciechowski) Sikorski 1953. bn, pf (a') (c.)

Bach, Johann Christoph Friedrich. Sonata in G major. (H. Ruf) BVK 1961. vc, bc (g') (c.)

————. Sonata in A major. (A. Wenzinger) BVK 1961. vc, bc (c′′) (c.)

Banner, Filippo. Sonata in G minor. (W. Upmeyer) Nagel 1957. (NMA 160) vc, pf (g′) (h.s.-c.)

Corrette, Michel. Sonata in D minor, Op. 20, No. 2. (H. Ruf) WMüller 1960. bn, bc (a′) (h.s.-c.)

dalla Bella, Domenico. Sonata in C major. (W. Upmeyer) Nagel 1960. (NMA 83) vc, pf (g′) (h.s.-c.)

Danzi, Franz. Concerto in F major. (R. Münster) Leuckart 1963. bn, pf (a′) (c.)

Eyck, Jacob van. Der Fluyten Lust-hof (Amsterdam 1646). (G. Vellekoop) Amsterdam, Ixijzet, 1957. 3 vols. unacc rec (treble clef: (a′′/c′′′) (c.)

de Fesch, Willem. 6 Sonate, Op. 8. (W. Schulz) Peters 1961. vc, bc (a♭′/a′) (h.s.-c.)

————. Sonata in D minor, Op. 13, No. 4. (H. Ruf) BVK 1959. vc, bc (g′) (c.)

Galliard, Johann Ernest. 6 Sonate. (J. Marx—E. Weiss-Mann) McG&M 1946. 2 vols. bn, pf (g′) (h.s.)

Gretchaninov, Alexander, et al. 6 Pieces. CMI 1955. 21 p. bn, pf (j.h.-h.s.) O/P

Hertel, Johann Wilhelm. Concerto in A minor. (H. Sallagar) Noetzel 1963. bn, pf (a′) (c.)

Marcello, Benedetto. 6 Sonate, Op. 2 [i.e. Op. 1]. (W. Kolneder) WMüller 1960. vc, pf (g′/a′) (c.)

Merci, Luidgi. Sonata in G minor, Op. 3, No. 4. (W. Bergmann) SchottL 1948. bn, pf (g′) (h.s.-c.)

Moffat, Alfred, comp. & arr. Old Master Melodies for Young Cellists. (E. Rapp) SchottL 1935. 27 p. vc, pf (j.h.)

————. Old Masters for Young Players. (P. Such) SchottL 1913. 27 p. vc, pf (g.s.-j.h.)

Pauer, Jirí. Capricci. Prague, SNKLHU (Boosey) 1953. bn, pf (b′) (h.s.-c.)

Picinetti, Felice Maria. Sonata in C major. (W. Upmeyer) Nagel 1965. (NMA 161) vc, bc (a′) (c.)

Schollum, Robert. Sonatine, Op. 55, No. 3 (1956). Doblinger 1957. bn, pf (a′/c′′) (c.)

————. Sonatine, Op. 57, No. 3 (1961). Doblinger 1963. bn, pf (c′′) (c.)

Stamitz, Carl. Concerto in F major. (J. Wojciechowski) Sikorski 1956. bn, pf (a′) (c.)

Torelli, Giuseppe. Sonata in G major. (F. Giegling) BVK 1964. (HM 69) vc, bc (f♯′) (h.s.-c.)

Vivaldi, Antonio. 6 Sonate. (W. Kolneder) SchottM 1958. vc, pf (g′/a′) (c.)

TUBA SOLOS

Beach, Bennie. Lamento. SouthernSA 1961. (f$\sharp$) (h.s.-c.)
Benson, Warren. Arioso. Piedmont 1959. (j.h.)
Bernstein, Leonard. Waltz for Mippy III. GSchirmer 1950. (e' — another version in Wekselblatt: g$\sharp$) (c.)
Beversdorf, Thomas. Sonata (1956). Interlochen 1958. (a) (c.)
Christensen, James. Ballad. Kendor 1963. (a/c') (h.s.)
Diercks, John. Variations on a Theme of Gottschalk. Tenuto 1968. (c')
    (h.s.-c.)
Hartley, Walter S. Sonata (1967). Tenuto 1967. (d$\flat$') (c.)
————. Sonatina (1957). Interlochen 1958. (a) (h.s.-c.)
————. Suite. Elkan-V 1964. unacc (b) (h.s.-c.)
Hindemith, Paul. Sonate (1943). SchottM 1957. (c') (c.)
Hogg, Merle E. Sonatina. Ensemble 1967. (d$\flat$') (c.)
Holmes, Paul. Lento. Shawnee 1961. (d') (h.s.-c.)
Kinyon, John, comp. & arr. Breeze-Easy Recital Pieces. Witmark 1958.
    32 p. (j.h.)
McKay, George Frederick. Suite for Bass Clef Instruments. Ann Arbor,
    Mich., University Music Press, 1958. (b) (h.s.)
Persichetti, Vincent. Serenade No. 12, Op. 88. Elkan-V 1963. unacc
    (e') (c.)
Phillips, Harry I., comp. & arr. 8 bel canto Songs. Shawnee 1967. 20 p.
    (j.h.-h.s.)
Presser, William. Rondo. Barnhouse 1966. (b$\flat$) (h.s.)
————. Suite. Ensemble 1967. unacc (c'/e$\flat$') (c.)
Schmidt, William. Serenade. Avant 1962. (c') (h.s.-c.)
Spillman, Robert. Concerto. EMusicus 1962. (f') (c.)
————. 2 Songs. EMusicus 1963. (e') (h.s.-c.)
Stevens, Halsey. Sonatina (1959-60). New York, Composers Facsimile
    Edition, 1960. (f') (c.)
Takács, Jenö. Sonata capricciosa, Op. 81. Doblinger 1967. (d') (c.)
Vaughan Williams, Ralph. Concerto. Oxford 1955. (e'/f') (c.)
Wekselblatt, Herbert. Solos for the Tuba Player. GSchirmer 1964.
    51 p. (h.s.) (solos by Bach, Bernstein, Mozart, Saint-Saëns, Shostakovitch, C. Stamitz, Tchaikovsky, and Wagner)

DATE DUE

JUN 1 1994			

GAYLORD PRINTED IN U.S.A.